T0015405

IT TAKES A
Worried
WOMAN

CRUX
THE GEORGIA SERIES IN
LITERARY NONFICTION

IT TAKES A
Worried
WOMAN

ESSAYS BY *Debra Monroe*

The University of Georgia Press
ATHENS

Published by the University of Georgia Press
Athens, Georgia 30602
www.ugapress.org
© 2022 by Debra Monroe
All rights reserved
Designed by Kaelin Chappell Broaddus
Set in 10.75/14.5 Kinesis Pro 3 Regular by Kaelin Chappell Broaddus
Printed and bound by Sheridan Books, Inc.
The paper in this book meets the guidelines for permanence
and durability of the Committee on Production Guidelines for
Book Longevity of the Council on Library Resources.

Most University of Georgia Press titles
are available from popular e-book vendors.

Printed in the United States of America
26 25 24 23 22 P 5 4 3 2 1

Library of Congress Control Number: 2022909648
ISBN: 9780820363080 (pbk.: alk. paper) ISBN: 9780820363097 (ebook)

For Shen, again

CONTENTS

1

Garnett and the Lavender-Lit Room   3
Unmarried: A Pastoral   17
The Makeshift Years   31
A Gendered History of My Hunger   46

2

Something New to Say about Domestic Violence   61
My Taciturn Valentine   72
Trouble in Mind   78
My Life as an Aeolian Harp   91
A Formal Feeling   99
The Wrong Conversations about Hate Activity   113

3

Last Home   129
Through the Bathroom Window at Dusk   139
The COVID Sunday Drives   148
Mistletoe   162

Acknowledgments   173

IT TAKES A
Worried
WOMAN

1

Garnett and the Lavender-Lit Room

A long-ago December I graduated from a small Wisconsin college a semester late, after my friends had left town for real jobs. None of them had
known me well, all of them acquainted with the fraction of my life that
had intersected with the fraction of theirs, maybe a class we once took or
an apartment we once shared. I began attracting the attention of women
old enough to be my mother, women whose maternal instincts no longer
had utility because their daughters lived far away or their relationships
had turned grievous.

I had cobbled together full-time employment and an incomplete in
Beginning Swimming, having postponed taking classes in Phys Ed until my final semester, when I had twenty credits, including two in Relaxation, in which I earned a C, and two in Beginning Swimming, which I'd
stopped attending. I'd floated the first day while the professor described
course goals, then fixed his eyes on me and said that anyone who already
knew how to swim had to switch to Advanced now. I obediently sank.
Late in the semester, bored by my excuse—a nearly Victorian account of
toiling for money on the wrong side of town, burning the candle at both
ends, studying while spent—he cut me a deal. He'd give me my diploma
after I spent twelve hours in the pool in January and February.

On Monday nights, I got into chilly water with inexplicably cheerful
people, bobbed for ninety minutes, then drove home in my warm coat,

gloves, and boots, wet hair wrapped in a bath towel, my swimming resti-
tution a temporary annoyance. I had bigger problems.

I discussed them with my neighbor, Bea.

I'd first introduced myself, waving from my sidewalk to hers, acting
warm yet unworldly, so she wouldn't worry about a college-age neighbor who might make her life harder with disdain or wild parties. She had
a sweet face and wore cardigans over flowered dresses—what my grandmother wore, not my mother in her color-coordinated knit slacks and
turtlenecks. My mother and Bea were in their forties. I was clueless, self-
absorbed. I thought they'd stopped aspiring and, sidelined, observed life
and remarked on it.

Bea agreed that the newspaper where I had two part-time jobs didn't
value my skill set. When I pressed for details about my marketable skills,
she cast about, vague compliments, and I understood she meant only that
she liked me, the way I admired her Catholic icons or her new yarn for
an afghan she was knitting. Bea said she'd been undervalued at Wool-
worth's, too, before quitting to raise her daughter, meaningful work until the world led the daughter astray. Sympathy was all she wanted on
the subject of her daughter, too painful. I told Bea I'd earned high praise
in college from a professor other students feared, an old-style academic,
originally from Mississippi, who insisted on research, and he read Eliza-
bethan sonnets with a southern accent. Bea asked why I didn't teach. I explained that I wasn't accredited. Education classes had seemed as dull as
Phys Ed.

Bea and her husband, Al, were kind, so I believed them when they
said the world won't pay us to do what we want to do, that hobbies and
love relieve us. Once, on the sidewalk, Al put his hand on his heart—soul-
ful eyes startling in his plain face—and said that love for Bea was his reason for working. Karl Marx's four alienations, which I read in school, described the life stretching before me, though Marx, unlike Bea and Al,
said that workers distract themselves with eating, drinking, and fornicating, not with love and hobbies.

Alienation from the Mode of Production. Al washed city vehicles after snow removal and trash pickup. Me, I'd beaten out journalism majors with my writing sample to get two jobs at one place. The internet didn't exist yet and cable TV was new. *Eau Claire Leader TeleCable* was the local newspaper's visionary-yet-not-quite-it idea of an electronic newspaper. Saturdays and Sundays, midnight until dawn, I pulled stories off the wire and condensed their content to the size of a TV screen. I transferred my abridged versions—the Hyatt-Regency walkway collapse, John Hinckley Jr.'s assassination attempt, protests against nuclear proliferation—into rotation on the newly launched station. People had a minute to read a story before it was replaced by another while easy listening music played. I read, wrote, clicked, changed easy listening reels every three hours.

That part of my job was unobjectionable. But four days a week, I pounded the pavement in Dress for Success outfits, skirted suits with blouses that had flowing bows, the female necktie, because career women were meant to look feminine-while-masculine but not feminist. I sold advertising spots that interrupted the easy listening, spots I wrote and produced, which is also why I beat out journalism majors. My voice, closer to tenor than alto, recorded well, and creative writing class had made the imitation of advertising easy: one-dimensional characters with faux-problems and faux-enthusiasm for touted solutions.

Alienation from the Product. I wasn't proud of my news stories because no one I'd met knew about the cable channel, and no one I knew heard my voice talking about hot sandwiches or snow tires in the midst of a prefab jingle. I had sales accounts. I was accountable. How avariciously fast I got at sifting the persuadable client from the unpersuadable, the persuadable someone who'd borrowed money and hung out a shingle, who hoped to be paid for doing what he liked. Olson Carburetor Repair. Clip Joint Barber. Jim's Meats. Small business owners bought my advertising because it was cheap, and they liked my heartfelt demeanor or, in quick time, the unctuous performance of this demeanor.

Alienation from Self. I hated myself now.

Alienation from Society. Weekends, condensing news, I'd wish the experienced reporter, an unhappy-looking woman who worked weekdays and smelled like booze at staff meetings, would get fired so I could take her place. I ignored my advertising client list. I went for long drives, developing furtive appreciation for the beauty of county highways in varying degrees of sun, rain, snow. I felt unethical filing my mileage reports, billing my employer for scenic time wasting. Yet convincing a business owner to buy useless advertising was unethical too. Meanwhile, the whole shebang was going under, as I could tell by the gloom in our office suite. One day, I called on an auto body shop and the owner praised the spot I'd produced, then said *Eau Claire Leader TeleCable* was a dumb idea and how about I replace his wife who was office bookkeeper and cleaned the shop bathroom.

With my weekends now free, I went out to hear music, Vern and the Roadhogs. Bikers with long beards liked this band. At a pig roast, a biker asked me to dance. I demurred, but later, a few sheets to the wind, I danced with a woman who hadn't gotten around to leaving town after college either. She worked full-time at what had been her part-time college job, supervising criminal teenage boys and—I'd told her how bad this sounded—she was attracted to one of her charges. As I refilled my cup at the keg, the biker with whom I'd declined to dance held the tap, his hurt expression unconcealed by a big beard: "You told me you didn't like dancing." Kindly or maybe ill at ease, I told him that the urge to dance overtook me. I simulated a friendly acquaintance with him, and, after he'd introduced them, with the other bikers too, his friends, now my friends. We didn't know each other well, just the part of our lives that intersected over Vern and the Roadhogs.

Hobbies. I started cooking.

Eating. I gained thirty-eight pounds in seven months.

I joined Weight Watchers, where I met several women old enough to be my mother. Members my age didn't last long. They'd join in small groups and, after they lost a pound or two, tell me they were celebrating by going out afterward to Dunkin' Donuts and invite me, and I'd decline, shocked. It wasn't their time to lose weight, an older member whispered: you have to want this for yourself. Older members dieted while shopping and cooking for hungry husbands. They deferred to Weight Watcher rules. I like rules, the promise of clear-cut results. I always wish for more rules, more results. When I arrived every Monday, older members smiled and waved. One cheered while I stood on the scale as my one- or two-pound weight loss would be announced. No one cared about my bad job, or that I'd attended wild parties, or that my only friend, who worked with criminal teenagers, was seedy. One would touch my long hair, a style she could no longer carry off, she said. Another liked my outfits in new styles, another a low-calorie recipe for stuffed perch I'd concocted. Mostly, they liked that I was happy to see them.

My sister still says that I was our mother's favorite.

My brother has always said our mother was mine.

He means I didn't like my father. I did try. But my father didn't like me. He loved me. He didn't want me to drown or die in a wreck. Yet even my runny nose, my allergies, upset him. My questions upset him. My brother or sister asked similar questions—are we going home yet? can we eat at Nick's Café?—and a fatherly moment ensued. Some kids are hard to take. Nervous. Talky. Standing too near when you don't want them. Or too far-off, making a trifling project from costly and vital household supplies, when you do. Once, his fist headed my way, I lurched to the floor, and he struck a light switch plate where, a moment earlier and inches away, my head had been. The light switch plate cracked and swung by a screw. My mother would never have let herself have favorites, though.

She was attuned to the moral fine print.

She talked about the difference between being good and seeming good. I wasn't her favorite, no, but she gave me extra attention, also chores like cooking or laundry that kept me from my father and my siblings, who, when they were kids, acquiesced to this idea that I was more hindrance than help. Unable to object to his scorn, she'd hoped to offset it. She also liked conversations to which I inclined, conversations about the ineffable, about what's caused and preventable versus what's happenstance and must be accepted.

Then my father left her for a younger woman. I was close to my goal weight and working at the auto body shop. I'd come home, ready to go back out again because I was fornicating the saxophone player from Vern and the Roadhogs. I'd find my mom waiting in her mint-green sedan. "I thought your door might be unlocked," she'd murmur, she who used to lecture about locking. She'd failed in an attempt to win my father back or felt unsatisfied by an act of revenge, for example going into his house, formerly hers, to unplug the freezer. By then, my dad's drinking was a small-town spectacle. I'd gone out to dinner with him and he'd shouted—maybe the restaurant seemed louder to him?—that the restaurant owner was ugly, bad acne, but at least he had a restaurant. Yet it hurts to be jilted.

One night, I canceled plans and phoned the seedy friend who also hadn't left town after graduation and now felt aberrantly close to a criminal teenage boy. I poured us all glasses of cheap wine and listened as my mother described anew her divorce sadness. My friend told my mother she should wear mascara and then a younger man would find her attractive.

In the yard one day, Bea told my mother I was sweet, and my mother seemed worried that Bea understood my secret worth. My sweetness, as my mother knew it, was buried under bluster and misdirection. The sweetness Bea knew was partly bluster and misdirection. To Bea and women at Weight Watchers, I showed part of my life, mistakes excised. This sounds premeditated, but self-presentation that won over a middle-aged woman missing her children was unforced, spontaneous. I wasn't alienated from *this* product.

At first, it's best to reveal to others and receive in return only what's self-flattering, self-protective, and keep the rest under wraps. Maybe because my father had told me not to talk, and my mother had told me not to talk to him, while making friends I'd say nothing. Then, like an inflated, not-yet knotted balloon slipping out of my hands and zooming away, my private theories and worries released. A few people responded well.

Not many, though.

The age difference between me and women old enough to be my mother asserted itself in ways small and large: different eras. The age difference meant I tempered my extreme revelations, as in: Does this mortifying incident I'm recounting mean I've wrecked my life? I relaxed, knowing if I failed with one there'd always be more. In time, I replaced caution with opinions I'd stopped testing. What they liked was piecemeal but unfaked.

Then the saxophone player introduced me to a bass player with a gentle facial expression. Or maybe it was aimless? He slept too much. He drank until he had flu-like hangovers. I pictured him energized by healthy meals and a schedule created by the job he'd get with the résumé I'd type, and he'd one day think, hand on his heart, that I was his reason for working. I married him. But he's not important. His mother is. She owned a fabric store and her grown daughters didn't sew. I'd needed a hobby to replace cooking, also new clothes as I lost weight. I'd started making colorful dresses, low-cost mood improvers.

My new mother-in-law and I had sewing conversations by phone even after I moved six hundred miles away to Kansas, bringing my new husband. He left me when we got to Kansas and took up with another woman. I'd moved for a scholarship, having learned that a master's degree would let me teach at a community college. I knew my mother-in-law would soon feel awkward about preferring phone calls with me to phone calls with her son. I'd need a replacement. I looked around for nearby Weight Watchers meetings.

I lived above the former general store in a village six miles from the university town where I was earning a degree and twenty miles from a town known for a storefront museum displaying memorabilia from *The Wizard of Oz*. Both had Weight Watchers meetings. Since I was killing time to avoid loneliness, I preferred a long drive through wheat fields to a short drive through wheat fields. I spent too much time in the university town anyway, in class, also rebranding myself as single. I'd befriended two female classmates, also single, also addressing crises of confidence but in a rebarbative way. One said to the other, but intended for me, about a botanical-print dress I'd sewn, "Leaves fell on her."

In a church basement in the small town, a woman with gray hair wheeled in the big scales. A stylish blonde old enough to be my mother's youngest sister unpacked files. The first woman said, "This is Weight Watchers. What do you want?" Even when I'd had weight to lose, I'd stood out at Weight Watchers, in which members' average age is forty-eight. Slender by then, only twenty-four, I quickly said, "I need to maintain my goal weight. I just moved here." The woman with the scales examined my Weight Watcher's Lifetime Membership card with its official seal and record of my pounds dropping. She shrugged. "Thirty-eight pounds is not nothing." More women old enough to be my mother arrived and, after I explained I'd lost weight and was now keeping it off, said welcome.

The gray-haired woman, Devita, soon asked if I'd collect fees while the stylish blonde weighed members. Devita had lost two times her body weight and drove four-hundred miles a week to lecture at meetings all over Kansas, where distance between towns is vast. The low pay, along with help from her husband, a mechanic, was enough to keep her car running. I'd get paid minimum wage, Devita said, but for no more than ninety minutes a week. This was not nothing. And I liked being in that church basement with women old enough to be my mother who described how they had or hadn't stayed on track, and Devita shouting, "Gals, don't skip on fat servings or you'll get the saggy skin."

They'd ask me if I was married or had a special fellow, and I'd say no, getting a divorce, and choke up, embarrassed and sad. Getting jilted even if you don't like the jilter is sad.

"What's wrong with him, then? Didn't know what he had."

"Happened to my daughter, hon. She's too huffy to know it yet, but she's better off."

Then we rushed off to watch one of the new nighttime TV shows in which the plot didn't wrap up every week, *Falcon Crest* with its better characters than *Dallas*, always trying too hard to flabbergast us, we'd agree, getting in our cars and waving goodbye.

I loved my landlady even more, Garnett, with her long black hair piled high like a 1960s film star. She had married sons with cordial wives because Garnett knew how to let go, she said, because daughters-in-law will always fight for control of their husbands. Garnett clashed with her oldest daughter too. I tried to make friends with Garnett's other daughter, my age, and single. Conversation fell flat. I delicately said so, and Garnett clamped her lips shut and said, "Tell me about it." Two days a week, Garnett opened the downstairs, the old general store with high ceilings and a pervasive smell of mice. It was filled with antiques and collectibles she'd bid on and stored in a barn until she bought the store.

On temperate days, Garnett and I sat outside on the bench or inside on rocking chairs. Midsummer through autumn, when Kansas is hot, we'd sit in a tin-lined room, the old walk-in cooler and, before that, storage for blocks of ice. We kept its door ajar to listen for customers, the tinkling bell when the big front door opened. The tin room was lit by grow-lights under shelves, once installed for marijuana cultivation, I suppose. Light reflected off the tin, and I felt quasi-religious, bathed in purple, as Garnett talked. If my mother had shared the same news, I'd have thought: oversharing! It would have been gritty details about my siblings, my father, and by then my scary stepfather, younger than my mother. I couldn't have listened without my own strong opinions, anger aroused and stirring.

I knew people Garnett talked about only by sight, though I now waved hello at one of her sons she'd once sent with a tractor to tow my car when I'd slid off the road in a blizzard. I began to recognize the expanding branches of her family tree, her mother, father, sisters, brother. Old memories she described entered me, old wounds merging with my wounds, memories spanning thirty years between us, events and conjecture, distinct yet blurry, known yet unfamiliar, like flocks of birds I'd once seen flying through clouds at dusk, confidences whirring through silence and prairie wind. I was her student, her understudy. I wanted to know how to make sense of life, which I thought she did and I would.

My habit of befriending these women, what got it started?

Just before I met Bea, toiling on the wrong side of town and missing Beginning Swimming at 8:00 a.m. because I got home from Meider's Lounge at 2:30 a.m., I drank to dull umbrage at customers I waited on while wearing the required clingy dress. Mr. Meider stared at barmaids and, his voice husky, said what he'd like to do to us. When his wife arrived, he stopped. I hovered near her. I said I loved how she'd done the décor, red carpet, black vinyl. We talked about vivid lipstick, which she wore and I liked but was out of style for women my age then. Stubbing out a cigarette, she said three of her kids were easy but didn't visit and the other was trouble. My boss, bored by the reminder that I was young enough to be his daughter, ignored then fired me but not until just before I graduated.

The first time was necessity then. But I got good at it.

I liked the eruption of unexpected mutual fondness.

Then Bea, then the Weight Watchers ladies, then Garnett.

The years ahead were leaner. I moved to Salt Lake City to earn a PhD, and my neighbor, who was Mormon and wore modesty clothing, looked old enough to be my mother but wasn't. Our conversation was about garbage pick-up times and her children, younger than me. I was in another marriage, bad from the start, with "red flags," as Dear Abby might say. If I'd met a woman old enough to be my mother who wasn't trying to convert me to her religion, a woman likely to share her secrets, for the foreseeable future I wouldn't share mine because you don't tell people you're in a bad marriage until it's over.

In North Carolina, I was an assistant professor and an older woman welcomed my arrival. She was one of those women, rare as a spotted owl, who'd earned a PhD in the 1950s. She said, "I was a tomboy, and they didn't know what to do." She said this a few times before I understood she wasn't calling herself a bluestocking who'd flummoxed colleagues at the start of her career but a lesbian. I never got to know her. I hid more than I showed. I obscured my worst detail, my marriage. A year later, when I moved to take a new job, I didn't tell her I was leaving my husband because even I didn't know until I'd gone.

I got to my new job and noticed Clara Mae when I went for walks.

One day, she asked me to look at a greenhouse her husband built by laying empty wine bottles in rows like bricks. "When people call a woman a 'free spirit' it sounds like a compliment, but they mean she has loose morals," she said once. "When people say 'how nice' they mean 'fuck you,'" she also said. With people she'd decided not to like, she'd say "how nice" and smile. This feisty and reflexive warding-off, incongruous because she looked like a sweet-faced old lady, was due to many years of having felt shunned, her only-child girlhood on the edge of the red-light district on Galveston Island, her job as a church secretary where church-goers didn't have senses of humor, and her two daughters had difficult husbands, one unemployed and lashing out, the other so good at making money he thought this meant he deserved the last say. At that time, I had no one. I once talked wistfully about how my mother used to make pork roast, and I came home from teaching the next day, and Clara Mae called. The table was set for me, pork roast.

One night the three of us—she, her husband, and I—went to eat at a café, her husband driving, Clara Mae across the seat from him, me slumped in back wearing old clothes, feeling contented as a kid and not a thirty-something professional. Clara Mae's husband took the last turn to home too fast, and we slid across our seats. Then the car straightened up and we did, laughing. Clara Mae smoothed her hair. "For God's sake, Debra," she said. "It's Saturday night. Even I think you should be doing something interesting."

Then I became a mother and, after many years of spooky phone contact only, my mother visited. Until her husband died, a heart attack, stroke of luck, it hadn't been safe to visit her, as I'd learned one night. She'd stood in the yard the next morning and asked me to go, better for both of us, and she never traveled without him. When she arrived for a visit, she asked to meet the nice old couple, my friends. Once, she was with Clara Mae and me, and my baby whose middle name is my mother's name because I'd wanted to plaster past the gap, symbolize over it. My mother watched me with Clara Mae, our inside jokes and casual talk. She looked sad she'd picked the company of her husband over mine. *Picked* isn't the right word. You marry while you're confused and get stuck, crushed.

These women were perhaps replacements for my mother.

True, I began to acquire them just as my familiar mother disappeared, and she disappeared as I'd begun my adult life, following a trail, tracing signs and footprints of women old enough to be my mother, but not my mother, so good sources for clues and hints I wanted. I don't mean my mother was a bad role model. These women weren't role models. I gathered scraps of knowledge flying this way and that as they described events in the past they'd managed or failed to manage. I didn't expect them to be strong or ideal, and I didn't act dutiful. We didn't have mutual trace resentments. I didn't slip back into a rusted-out old version of myself, petulant child, moody adolescent, impatient teenager, and they didn't feel obliged to nag me about a life skill I hadn't mastered yet, neither of us offering advice in the eye of the storm, advice too soon, wrong advice, unwelcome advice.

Loving my mother was harder, though I did love her.

Clara Mae was a bad sleeper who took various pills. Each one, over time, would stop working. One day, I saw an ambulance in the driveway.

EMTs shouldn't have answered my question: "What's happened, what's happened?" But one of them did: "Psychiatric episode." Code for overdose. I visited her in the hospital. She'd taught me names of wildflowers and obscure verses to folk songs. In the hospital, she could barely talk, but we recited wildflower names and, as a puzzled nurse walked in, we sang the second sorrowful verse to "On Top of old Smokey." When she came home, I brought meals a few times a week. My mother died that winter. A few weeks later, Clara Mae died too.

I now do without them or anyone like them for the rest of my life, without a woman a generation older to whom I unloose my fears and hopeful guesses, without an ardent friendship that, like most friendships, was performed at first, shame or pain summarized into euphemism or witty versions of typical rites of passage because granular details of shame or pain are best told after love and assent are well-established, deep roots.

But the habit of looking persists.

I have good friends my own age, nearby and spread across the country. I'm fine in a crowd but better one on one, deciding whether to trust, the lingering uncertainty I'm more hindrance than help. And my profession, teaching, means I'm the elder, sharing experience, acquired skill. I've been happy working, not alienated from my product or process or self or society, as many are, my father, for instance, nursing dissatisfaction while nursing drinks for decades. But sometimes I want someone nearby who doesn't expect evidence I'm hale, happy, wise. The habit of looking returns when I'm close to home because I discovered Bea next door, Garnett downstairs, Clara Mae around the corner. But I live in a city now. You're not supposed to talk too long to your neighbors. If you need friends, as Dear Abby says, you join a club. Like Weight Watchers, I think. But no.

Because I garden, I noticed the well-tended yard down the street first and the gray-haired woman who tended it next. One day, we talked about her canna lilies. She was a retired English teacher, she said. I'm an English teacher, I said. Then the conversation stalled.

After I left Kansas, I wrote to Garnett for a few years and she wrote back, her spindly handwriting on flowered stationary. I searched her name on the internet and found a newspaper notice in the small town with the storefront museum, posted by her daughters last year, asking for cards for Garnett's ninetieth birthday. If I'd known I'd have sent a card, mine falling into many, hiding the surprise after thirty-some years of no contact, her daughters maybe reading the cards aloud and not remembering me or, if they did remember me, wondering how I'd seen the notice. I assume Garnett once in a while thinks of me. I remember her when I'm in a quiet store and the bell at the front door chimes just so, when wind howls fiercely, when low clouds at dusk turn the sky luminous purple.

The gardening gray-haired neighbor invited me to her church on the other side of the city, worth the drive, she said. I'd slipped into the old pose, a younger, less-knowing woman bereft of insight. We exchanged phone numbers and promised to chat. Now when I'm walking and see her, I wave uneasily because it's not her fault she's not old enough and I'm not young enough to re-create that duet of comfort, one of those friendships in which advice was never the point, a friendship in which the two of us welcomed each other, our faces lighting up, our affection lighting up the shared search for direction in the overlapping portion of our lives we knew better than anyone else, intimacy fractional but great.

Unmarried: A Pastoral

I doubled the size of the cabin, making it into a house. Then my former front door led to the kitchen, which seemed wrong. So I added a second door leading to the new living room. I took as inspiration well-ventilated houses built before electricity—old houses with many doors, many porches. I had my back porch for eating meals in shade. My front porch, wide open to the sky, was for solitary thinking on the porch swing. People visiting sometimes said *wonderful, two porches!* Also, *odd, two front doors!* But people didn't often visit. One night, rain-scented wind whipped through the back porch, the back door, out the two front doors. All three screen doors slapped and rattled as I sat on the front porch with a man. We'd just made love in my bedroom. Now we were eating mangoes.

The air, muggy-steamy for weeks, turned suddenly fresh. In the dark, I couldn't see leaves on trees and plants and spears of grass, all fatigued by hot summer, ready for rain. I looked through the lit-up rectangle of the door to my living room, at a staircase I'd sanded and stained myself. It led to a loft designed for nothing but the luxury of space to sew while my daughter played nearby. In a room below the staircase, door ajar, night-light aglow, my daughter slept. I'd lived alone in the country a long time, then with my daughter, and then my daughter got her first pet, a kitten on the other side of the kitchen's slapping screen door, her head tilted, cat-curious about the wind, the doors, the changing weather.

———

I'd sat on that porch swing with a few men a few times before, not many.

A middle-aged couple who lived down the road would beg to differ.

Passing by in their truck, they'd somehow always see the visiting car in my driveway. The next day I'd leave to run errands, and this couple, somehow always running errands, too, would stop, unroll windows, heads tilted, neighbor-curious. The husband: "You had company." The wife: "One of her boyfriends." I'd smile: "A dinner guest."

I did sometimes cook meals for these men I let inside after my daughter was asleep. Then I ushered them back out. Most never got past the initial phone calls and final screening, lunch in the city. They all came highly recommended, not for what I lacked, a life of the body to complement the life of the mind and spirit, no. For being not sketchy. For being good company. A previous man I'd sat with on the porch swing—before the night of the mangoes, fresh wind, and quizzical kitten behind the slapping screen door—was an architect who'd designed and built a house for two of my friends, married to each other. The wife: "I picture you talking about your shared interest, building houses." *Something there is that doesn't love a wall, that sends the frozen groundswell up under it,* Robert Frost. Something there is that doesn't love a single woman either. I mean I told my friend I was mostly interested in the sex, and she'd rolled her eyes.

These men, fresh out of relationships they'd assumed would last, seemed hard-pressed to remember how they'd once done courtship, the light banter. If they'd been on a dating website, they'd have checked a box: *looking for friendship, maybe more.* I wanted the *more* with pleasant conversation before and after. I'd made life compartments, partitions. Biology wants to breach them. If sex is good, your body produces dopamine (happiness), serotonin (relaxation), and oxytocin (bonding). Happiness and relaxation are good. Bonding expressed as tenderness is good. But happy and relaxed bonding means it's easy to put into words feelings that aren't true and likely won't ever be, premature endearment.

When I'd sat with the architect on my porch swing, he, too, looked through the lit-up rectangle of my living room door at the staircase I'd sanded and stained. He praised it. Who knows if his compliment was sincere, since house design was his profession. But he was chockful of oxytocin, involuntary tenderness. He liked how the stairs went two steps to a landing, then veered, also the rippling look of the balusters. Who drew my house plans? Sketched, I said. I did. Then I'd hired a carpenter, a roofer, an electrician, a plumber. I'd done the painting and staining. I'd had a budget, also abiding interest in my walls.

Good lovemaking doesn't happen right away. People say that. I wouldn't know. I never waited to find out. Sometimes it does happen right away. Sometimes, when I was young and less careful, I'd find myself in the happy and relaxed aftermath (bonding or its illusion) with a difficult person. The extricating, the divorce, took years. That night, rain fell, and the architect put his arm around me and said: "Turn off that bourgie water feature, why don't you? So we can listen to the rain." He meant turn off the submerged pump in a fishpond with waterfall I'd helped build, discovering my latent talent for stirring cement, placing rocks. When the architect first arrived at dusk, I'd shown him my yard, enclosed by a fence I'd had built. Then I'd planted thick vines over it. Yet the middle-aged couple somehow always peered into my driveway. I also showed him the arbor I'd had built, a freestanding porch under tall trees. And my fishpond with falling water.

In retrospect, I'm not crazy about the fishpond.

A hulking guy I'd hired to build the fence first suggested it. I'd been enamored of other people's fishponds, unaware that fishponds took such work, such maintenance. Nothing worth having is easy. People say that too. Every spring, I moved the lily with heart-shaped leaves and red blooms into clean water, the goldfish into clean water, and then I bailed the old water and scrubbed, hours of toil, while my daughter asked lively questions.

"Your little girl might enjoy feeding some goldfish," the hulking guy working on my fence had said. These projects lasted months, and he'd ask to come inside and use my restroom (you can't fight nature); if my daughter's father paid child support (a too personal line of inquiry I cut short by pointing out she was adopted and I was single); if I found it hard to raise a Black child in a mostly White, rural setting (a paraphrase: "a kid like that out here"). This question was also too personal. But it cut to the heart of my dilemma, that the countryside and nearby village weren't optimal for a single woman, let alone a White one whose child was Black. But I'd already fortified, made my perimeters strong.

My daughter did like feeding goldfish, differentiating between them, giving them names based on how boldly or cautiously each one vied for food. But after I'd gone and built the fishpond with fountain, a faraway friend with a PhD in literary theory flew into one of the airports over an hour away and came to visit. We sat in my arbor, drinking wine, and she said, "I don't suppose you notice you've put a vatic symbol smack-dab in the middle of your yard, like a man with his tower or silo." A vatic symbol is the inverse of a phallic symbol. From *vates*: deep well, source of mystery and wonder. Symbolism, once seen, I couldn't unsee. Yet, from the porch, I liked the melodious sound, that night merging with rainfall.

I didn't want to walk through pouring rain to turn off the pump, and the architect, jokey and affectionate too soon, prematurely, had made fun of my landscaping. All the preparatory phone calls and final screening, the lunch date, had led to surging relaxation for him but not for me. Good lovemaking would have taken time. My schedule, synced with my daughter's, was fixed. I mentioned the late hour. I stood. Water falling in a fountain is for fish, I told him. Fish need aeration, I added. He looked nervous. I never let him inside again.

I saw him two years later, across a restaurant. By then, my daughter litigated her bedtime. "The sky is light," she'd maybe say. I'd answer that the sun set later in summer due to nature, the earth tilting, and culture, daylight saving time, and send her back to bed. Through her open door, she'd call for me to look out her window at the half-light and beautiful shadows and biggest stars shining before the sky gets all the way black, and this went on. It had been easy enough to say to a friend of my friends that I could see him after my daughter was asleep if I meant 9:00 p.m. It was odder to say I'd see him at 10:00 or 11:00, and even odder to say that I barely had daycare let alone nightcare, that I didn't spend time with anyone if this was time subtracted from time I'd spend with her, that I wanted only late-night sex, a too terse summary. I wanted late-night good sex with a kind man.

Unintended scarcity effect: people want what's in short supply. A man to whom I'd said *goodbye, goodnight, see you in three weeks*, usually hoped to see me in a few days.

I deferred the life of the body.

Until another friend, a faraway city-dwelling early adopter of new technology who thought I was crazy to live in the country while single, suggested another man. Dating websites were new. The internet was, too, my connection to it wheezing and dial-up. Whenever she couldn't sleep, she searched for men within fifty miles of me. She made a profile for me and described how to log on. The introduction was modern. But meeting up was not. I began to observe the custom of the country. Though my goal was going to bed, not prom, I started "dating." Dating includes social interaction in broad daylight. I'd be holding my daughter's hand, walking down the road, conversing with a man, and the middle-aged couple in their truck stopped, smiled, hunches about a car in my driveway confirmed.

When I saw the architect in a restaurant that night, I was with the chief technical officer of a company called Encryptic, also his daughter, age twelve, and my daughter, age three. The architect didn't notice me. He gazed into a woman's face. She gazed back. Everyone finds someone, people say. My friend had picked the CTO for me because she liked that he was French. She saw us having cross-cultural conversations about shared interests.

One shared interest was food. We both liked eating, and he knew recipes I'd otherwise never have learned. And all the *caveat emptor*, the phone calls and the final screening, lunch in the city, led to surging relaxation for both of us. He began to describe our future, how and where it would take place. I thought: never and nowhere, too tricky. My job, his job, my house, his house, my daughter, his daughter. I anticipated only the looming extrication as, worried, I let him inside my well-tended walls, and he became a fixture in my daughter's life, inadvertent influence, intermittent role model, when all I'd screened him for was potential with regard to the life of the body and the before-and-after conversation.

We resorted to comparing French and American mores. He'd describe all he did and felt as typically French, which couldn't have been true because all I did and felt wasn't typically American. Each weekend, he'd pick up his daughter at the house of his ex-wife's new husband, the CTO's former best friend, and when the CTO got to my house with his daughter, he'd say he felt tenderness about his ex-wife, also jealousy, a French attitude, he said, his face flickering sadness. According to American custom, he was in love with his ex-wife. According to American custom, I should have minded, yet I didn't.

We'd take our daughters to a mall for shopping, to a lake for a hired boat ride, to a river for swimming. Our failsafe date, bowling, became a shared interest. My daughter liked giving the child's pink ball the heave-ho. His daughter liked hurling the teen's glittery red ball. Bowling is an ancient and international game, he said. I pointed out it used to be played in the United States on communal outdoor greens and that's why a few U.S. cities are named Bowling Green. He replied, amiable, that in France *boules* is still played outdoors.

Late at night, when my daughter was sleeping and his daughter was watching rented movies, we sat on my porch swing, and he drank glass after glass of wine, a typical rate of consumption in France, he said. He told me about his past. To remember is to interpret. To remember again is to reinterpret. A detail that once seemed crucial falls away, and new details merit new attention. Or you felt troubled or impatient then but curious or dispassionate now, this retelling. But more than his perspective changed during retellings.

He'd joined the navy when he was sixteen, making the navy his legal guardian. Or he didn't, and his grandmother was his guardian then. His mother was either a prostitute or a band groupie. He was or wasn't in the French Special Forces. He shouldn't be telling me any of this because it was all a personal or state secret. Every few weeks, when his cellphone rang in the middle of the night—I had a landline that bleated nondescriptly, no middle-of-the-night bleating because middle-of-the-night phone calls are considered rude in America—his eerie ringtone overtook, first, my dreams, and then the sound of wind stirring trees outside my wide-open windows, and the call would be his ex-girlfriend, no, friend.

Inconsistencies manifested at night as my fishpond with its rocky outcropping burbled. In the morning, as our daughters watched cartoons in the living room, we ate breakfast on the back porch, eggs scrambled with leeks, salmon, creamy cheese, a French recipe. I'd ask for clarification. He'd drunk too much, he'd say. *Le vin entre, la raison sort.*

Pleasant moments entangle you. Unpleasant hours, days, weeks disentangle you. Late-night assignations end quickly as you spoil the good mood, maybe on purpose. But "dating" can go on too long because, just when you're on the verge of an ultimatum, you're tranquil again because he has to leave to go to work or return his daughter to her mother's.

He started arriving alone in the middle of the week. Once, during a weather event, a flood, he stayed for three days and nights. The sky rained, rained, rained, extravagant. We sat on the porch swing in the dark and listened to the downpour, downspouts rushing into runnels, the rushing fountain running into the fishpond, the fishpond rushing out, running over. Daytime: meals, music, card games. Nighttime, when my daughter slept, we sat on the porch. Roads were impassable. On Monday, the sun rose bright and solid, and he drove away. I looked at my yard, glistening, blinking, glimmering, and unfamiliar with overgrowth, the leaves heavy with water, branches bent, then straightening up again, normal.

A few weeks later, I sat in a chair on one end of the front porch, and the CTO sat on the porch swing. His daughter came outside. My daughter was climbing into my lap. The CTO was on his cellphone, arguing with his ex-wife. He cast the phone aside, complaining about the attenuated signal, degraded reception. I said something vague. The CTO's daughter sighed dramatically, made eye contact with her father, flicked her head at me, and rolled her eyes. Her mother and father argued in front of her. She did and didn't like her new stepfather, depending on how you asked. She no doubt did and didn't like me. Almost imperceptibly, the CTO sighed too, rolled his eyes, and smiled back at her, concurring. I assumed—correctly, because he broke up with me—that he felt as bored with me as I was with him and "dating" that had lasted too long. Dropped signals, both of us.

People tend to see a woman and child without a man as a last-resort arrangement, including friends who suggested this or that man, or the hulking guy who thought I'd been deserted by the baby's father, or neighbors who counted cars in my driveway, trying to decide if I was depraved or unlucky. I wasn't immune to cues and signs. I understood that if I felt the sex urge I'd be better off treating it as the marriage urge. I resisted, trying to keep my life partitioned: solemn responsibilities here and my recurring, angsty desires there.

Neighbors in a city with many social encounters per day, sheer overload, will give you privacy and expect it back. Neighbors in the country, isolated, with so few social encounters per day, offer up personal details, hoping for interaction. Joyce, a woman in a sunhat who sometimes wandered by on foot, had earned a PhD in biological psychology after her children were grown. She earned the degree as a hobby, she told me, because she'd inherited her money. One day, I met her husband, a short, wide man, almost handsome, whose main hobby seemed to be keeping tabs on people who parked outside the lines in grocery store parking lots. He left them notes on their windshields. The next time I saw Joyce, she said, "By now we've worked out what not to talk about, you see. I had children at home when I met him. I was in a peaking emergency—a woman in my thirties." She shook her head, remembering. "I didn't understand the sexual physiology yet, the data."

Men I met would explain their interests to me, and I'd explain mine to them. For instance, the CTO once noticed student essays on my desk about a story I'd taught, "Kew Gardens" by Virginia Woolf. In it, nature can't be separated from the formal garden, built to contain it. A metaphor: human sexuality can't be separated from marriage, built to contain it. Couples stroll "before smooth pink folds of the flower burst their gummy case," through "heart-shaped or tongue-shaped" leaves, flowers with red and blue tips, pistils "rough with gold dust and slightly clubbed at the end." This imagery is like Georgia O'Keeffe's first drawings, exhibited in 1916, that she didn't seem to realize looked like wombs with fallopian tubes. The art critic Willard H. Wright said, "These pictures say 'I want to have a baby.'" Art critic Henry McBride said: "Even advanced art lovers felt a distinct moral shiver."

Among Virginia Woolf's oval flowerbeds, couples feel wild urges but stay on tame paths leading them to be with others, leading them to conformity, to marriage, because to want undomesticated nature, to want nature outside of culture, is to risk madness and shunning because the normative path won't permit deviation, which is to say that sex outside of marriage, especially with a child asleep in another room, is a deviant deviation. I didn't say all that to the CTO who'd read a student essay, frowned, and said: "So this is the study of literature?" I said, "We talk about implied meaning, yes. But it's not all sex and flowers."

I mostly never made it to "dating," stalled out on the awkward phone calls or lunch in the city, all the garbled and confusing talk, colliding mindsets, our self-contained preoccupations, our sequestered vocabularies. A friend set me up with her husband's friend, who had a master's degree in business administration. We had one phone call, then lunch. The logic of the stock market, which would be fascinating and helpful to understand, eluded me. People did or didn't understand it, the MBA told me, impatient. He sighed and said, "Books are all well and good, Debra, but money makes the world go around."

Another friend asked if she could give my phone number to her husband's friend, an abstract expressionist painter who'd relocated to the nearby city and hoped to meet a woman. I wondered: didn't abstract expressionism end in the 1970s? During the first and only phone call, I learned that abstract expressionism did mostly end in the 1970s, and that he was way too old for me. What had my friend been thinking? I didn't get to ask before she told me he'd found me "provincial." My out-of-state friend who whiled away insomnia by searching dating websites for men within fifty miles of me suggested a graphic designer whom I met for lunch. He stared so long at my moving mouth as I spoke—no, at my lipstick, I realized midsentence—I began to worry its hue was wrong. A biologist studied bats but talked about breeding dogs. A paleontologist confessed he wasn't really a paleontologist. This was another conversation hurdle: poetic license, false advertising.

If I sound dispassionate now, describing "dating" and all its toil, at the time I'd internalized the default explanation: I was too picky. Except when I wasn't. Sometimes, when I was younger and getting divorced, or older and I found someone appealing and then didn't, a breaking-point accumulation leading to a break-up, friends or neighbors volunteered that they'd seen warning signs before I had. Then, apparently, I hadn't been picky enough. All my willpower couldn't conjure love. With gender roles like templates, heterosexual love is hard to remodel. You can add on and rearrange, but it was long ago designed to give women less autonomy and say-so. I had my wishes and blind spots. I swam upstream.

I'd feel fine about my alternative plan until desire reasserted, a biological fact, a peaking emergency. Then I'd reconsider my location, my walls and fences, my open door framing a staircase leading to space for just me with my child. I hadn't cleared a path toward the respected and permanent solution, marriage. Courtship leading straight into marriage is a way to have sex that won't attract undue attention from your neighbors. Joyce in her sunhat: "I had children. Needing sex was too distracting. I had to find a way to stay in at night."

On the night of the fresh wind and quizzical kitten behind the slapping screen door, I'd verified that the man with whom I was eating mangoes hadn't so far lied or even exaggerated. I had broadband connection by then, and I'd found the website for the agency where he worked, also a newspaper article in which he'd answered a reporter's questions about an archaic law not yet overturned. At the final screening, lunch, not in the city but at a bland restaurant on the highway halfway between the man's house and mine so I wouldn't drive further than him, and this was his idea, I'd told him I loved my child more than I could love a man, no contest, final opinion. He understood. His son came first.

This exchange cleared the way for late-night good sex to come, the X-factor potential for which you can't ascertain by way of friends' enthusiasm for the match, nor through online research, due diligence. But you might sense it, far-off lightning, a muted clap of thunder, even while standing on a sidewalk leading into a bland restaurant halfway between houses.

At the lunch date, which was also my daughter's first day of first grade, we decided to see each other late at night every third weekend. He said that since he was a single parent part-time and I was a single parent full-time, he'd assume more of the driving. But our plans accelerated, due in part to one of those times when raising a Black child in a mostly White, rural setting turned out to be hard. As soon as school started, my daughter said her teacher was mean. On Meet the Teacher Night, I'd noticed the teacher was unjolly, at least with us. But she didn't know us yet, I'd reasoned. On the fifth day of school, my daughter begged not to go. I asked why. Nothing she said made sense.

She told me the teacher sent her to stand in the hall twice because she'd asked for a hug twice because other kids got hugs. The teacher had said not to ask, not now, not later. Asking for a hug could be pushy and disruptive, I reasoned. Yet my daughter's kindergarten teacher had given her high marks on the part of the report card covering age-appropriate socialization. I wondered if the new teacher was racist, then stopped myself, such extreme guesswork without evidence. Then my phone rang. A parent who volunteered at the school called to tell me that the teacher complained about my daughter while complaining about "the Blacks," all of them. And, the parent-volunteer said, even if she hadn't, over and over reducing the same student to tears in front of her classmates is wrong.

Three weeks after lunch at the bland restaurant, not yet a week after mangoes on the porch swing, the man phoned me to ask how my day was. I'd met with the teacher during her free hour to say I was concerned my daughter didn't like school. She said my daughter was spoiled. I said she'd done well in kindergarten. This teacher scoffed: the kindergarten teacher was a pushover! I met with the principal next. The parent-volunteer had said not to quote her, so I stuck to three talking points: my daughter had done well in kindergarten; this teacher and my daughter were a bad fit; this teacher had sent my daughter into the hall twice. "Unattended?" the principal asked. I was still deciding how to say, without proof, that the teacher might be racist when the principal said we'd meet with the teacher at four. At the meeting, the teacher said I was playing "the race card," yet I hadn't mentioned race, and the principal told her that sending a child to the hall was against policy.

This is a lot to tell a man you've had sex with just once.

But I kept on. By then, it was late, I told him. People locking up, going home, and I'd gone home, and my daughter went to bed, worried about school. I'd promised to make sure the teacher wasn't still mad, an impossibility, because she was madder, and I needed to keep the principal amenable because this was only first grade, many grades to come. I said all this into my first cellphone as I sat on the porch swing looking at the night sky, and the man on the phone with his degree in jurisprudence, ingrained sense of fairness, and expertise in crafting best solutions with the least fallout, suggested tactics and word choices, not unlike tactics and word choices I'd used and considered using, but I was in the midst of my trouble, second-guessing myself, compensating for my presumed worry-distortions.

I got my daughter moved to a new classroom the next morning.

It wasn't that all the walls came down, but he started staying over every Friday and appearing in my sun-bright driveway on Saturday mornings. The middle-aged couple first waved, then stopped their truck, got out, ambled over, introduced themselves, asked him where he lived and worked. He politely answered, a suitor passing muster with village elders.

We drove back and forth between our houses for four years. Then my daughter and I moved to the city, into a house spacious enough for a blended family. I stepped into my place in the pattern. Marriage has institutionalized legal benefits. Its social benefits are harder to quantify. But I noticed that a difference of opinion with a handyman or one of my daughter's teachers was resolved quickly if I made my point with a husband nearby. He didn't think he had this superpower until we were at one of my stepson's events with my husband's ex-wife, and I said the PTA president was rude, haughty, and my husband said he'd noted only graciousness, and my husband's ex-wife laughed and said he hadn't believed her either when she'd told him the PTA president yelled at mothers and flattered fathers.

But that first night I sat with him on the porch swing, a woman without a husband, a fish without her bicycle, I was thinking only that good sex and its euphoric aftermath aren't love. Even if they are, I probably reminded myself, I didn't like love's one-size-fits-all blueprint, marriage. I couldn't see that marriage would ever be big enough. I couldn't see that in less than a week the man would help me solve a dicey problem at my daughter's school, nor that in the months and years ahead we'd almost always agree about life's big occasions and crises, nor that my daughter would love him as his son would love me. I heard rain rumbling, the fishpond fountain pumping, and wind rushing. My daughter's kitten darted its tiny head in and out of the slapping screen door, and a gust blew through the house, filling it, then out the screen door next to me, which slapped quickly shut, and the kitten was almost killed but wasn't. She eventually became an old cat blinking in the lap of an old man across a roomy room from a contented old woman, me. I didn't foresee any of that.

The Makeshift Years

For ten years, I was a single parent, not the first, last, nor only. Because I adopted, my ideas, my house, my character, and my income were assessed in advance by experts. I planned ahead for likely setbacks, and the adoption agency doublechecked. Preemptive problem-solving is a skill and a tic. On one hand, it's planning, and planning helps. On the other, no one can anticipate all future bad luck or glaring miscalculations always obvious after the fact. Still, as I waited for my baby, I envisioned upcoming hurdles: my worrying and readying and rushes of elation as I'd clear them. I've daydreamed like this since I can remember, with naiveté or hubris or willed faith in my ability to spot looming hazards.

The elementary school principal later said: "No ex-husband, no grandma, no aunt, not even an uncle?" My extended family was geographically afar. I visited rarely and called often. Geographically afar worked: unfixable history and latent eruptions, even by phone. So I began as a mother who hoped to forestall all problems but then saw my daughter emerging into consciousness with the suspicion that, if push came to shove, no one else would love her, feed her, and save her. She asked often about her contingency plan.

She was sick when she was little, which I did foresee, that a child might have special needs. Hers were appointments with medical specialists in a city an hour away. But a problem I didn't foresee was that I would get sick.

One day, she was wearing cozy pajamas and watching TV. I lay on the couch, wondering why nurses rushed me when I phoned to say I hadn't recovered from surgery yet. My daughter said, "How will Aunt Cindy"— a friend in Florida, and we lived in Texas—"know to come on a plane and get me?"

I thought: some fantasy about going to Disneyworld?

"When you die," she said. She'd arranged her expression to convey that she needed this information but knew I was overextended. She also knew I'd traveled to my mother's funeral, that the mother of her sitter had died a good death at home in the room near the room where she napped and played. "I'm not dying," I said, ignoring my post-op malaise.

Caregivers had a finite interest in her. They worried about their own children, their own mothers. None were terrible, though one seventeen-year-old had bulimia. I could tell by the candy wrappers and the state of the bathroom. I wondered whether to tell her mother, whom I'd first met when the mother was a childcare worker at a Methodist Church program called Mother's Day Out, which I'd used for daycare when my daughter was two. You left your child there—Tuesdays, Thursdays, 9:00 to 3:00, steep fines if you were late for pickup—to relax or shop. The childcare worker who turned out to be the sitter's mother told me she knew by my clothes I was going to work at the university in the college town a half-hour away. I couldn't use daycares there. My hours were erratic, midday classes Tuesdays and Thursdays, also a Thursday night class requiring a second arrangement.

"The church board is strict," she said. "Be discreet."

I nodded and tried to seem on the verge of shopping.

This was another problem I'd failed to foresee. I owned a small house near a visually appealing village with a low cost of living, but it had just one daycare center that everyone described as dodgy, in a pole barn between the dancehall and auto body shop. Social workers must have assumed I'd devise childcare. I did. Here are maxims I lived by:

- Impatience is a virtue. It helps you get chores done quickly.
- Worry is precaution.
- If you predict bad outcomes, you'll have spare solutions stockpiled.
- Wait, wait. We're almost at the palace. It's not midnight. Something good will still happen. (This began as an ironic aside but, after long repetition, turned sincere.)

When at last my daughter was enrolled in all-day kindergarten, I needed just one sitter one night a week for night class. I said this when I ran across the Mother's Day Out childcare worker, who'd suggested I enroll my daughter in Saturday morning ballet classes in the city an hour away, expensive yet excellent classes she'd heard. Surely I wasn't working on Saturday mornings? Then she said I should hire her daughter who had a car.

I hired the daughter and discovered the bulimia. My habit of misgiving tumbled onto a new question: was it my place to tell the sitter's mother about the bulimia? Telling the mother might be wrong, thankless. This was an etiquette question, I realized. Etiquette is about conveying difficult facts kindly. Next I had to fire the sitter for not picking up my daughter—leaving my daughter's small, dear self at the top of a hill where the school bus dropped her. One of my neighbors other neighbors called Crabby Old Man, but never to his face, drove her back to school where the principal called me at work, and I rushed out of a seminar in which I let students keep their cell phones on, a new gadget then, because I couldn't object to theirs if, alert to predicaments, I kept mine on.

After I found a new sitter, I found myself oddly missing the previous nonurgent question of whether I should tell the sitter's mother her daughter wasn't okay. Next I pondered why I'd found the question mildly intriguing. I'd rolled it over in my mind as I drove to and from work, as I vacuumed and folded laundry, as I'd answered my daughter's questions about who made the sky and were animals people, as I'd helped her with her kindergarten homework, easy, fun, the two of us pasting feathers onto a drawing of a turkey for Thanksgiving or reading aloud a list of seasonal words as I quelled panic about how supervising her homework would get harder in years ahead, taking up more focus.

I probably never would have found the spare courage to tell the sitter's mother about her daughter's eating disorder, which was concerning. A warning about the sitter's well-being. A warning about the sitter's fitness. Something to keep an eye on. But not a firing offense, not yet, I must have decided, coming home from teaching at 10:00 p.m. to empty the wastebaskets and clean the bathroom. Problem-solving in a pros-versus-cons way had turned reflexive. Thinking about someone else's problem, hard for them but easier for me, had felt like a pastime. Mother's Day Out had the right idea—I needed to relax. But any new pastime had to overlap with time I'd spend with my child. Maybe gardening?

The next sitter picked up my daughter right at the school, along with the sitter's daughter who was the same age, and at 10:00 p.m. I'd drive to this sitter's, heading north off my route home, otherwise western, then south again home, twenty extra miles but just one night a week. This sitter was affectionate, big-hearted, with a dry sense of humor, but she'd just begun taking an antidepressant, the first rough weeks of adjusting to a drug. When I knocked on the door to pick up my daughter, this sitter was disturbingly hard to wake.

Don't worry about keeping my sitters straight. Think of them as members of a fractious Greek chorus, contradicting each other while letting spill with advice derived from their circumstances, different from mine. But I had to value them as individuals since I needed them to value my daughter. I didn't treat them as interchangeable as they interchanged.

I slept lightly and woke often, and my dreams were as busy as action movies. I'd be driving home but couldn't decipher the infinitely branching roads just beyond the windshield. Or I was in an unfamiliar city, wide expressways crisscrossing before me like lines in an M. C. Escher lithograph.

In one dream, my car wouldn't start. So I stole a motorcycle, kickstarted it, and sped off, one hand steadying the baby draped over the gas tank. I woke, relieved to find myself in bed, my child asleep, nowhere I had to be for two hours.

Linear time was my roadmap. Monday Tuesday Wednesday Thursday (different due to night class), Friday again. Saturday and Sunday unstructured but full of to-dos. Weekdays, 7:00 a.m., 8:00, 9:00, 10:00. . . Starting at 4:00 p.m. on weekdays except Thursdays: meet the school bus, fix a snack, see to homework, chat happily, fix dinner. We ate. She bathed. For TV, she liked physical comedy, extravagant pratfalls. I'd be in the next room, washing dishes, and hear her helpless with laughter, chortling. On weeknights, *America's Funniest Home Videos*. Saturday, British comedies like *Fawlty Towers*.

I now see that, despite daily progress—the clock mapping my day, the calendar mapping my week and, panning outward for a disorienting minute, my month—I'd get stuck. Any intersection with a forking set of options, with more than one way forward, possibly two, three, or four, all potentially the right or wrong way, unsettled me. Friendly landmarks looked strange. I mean those talisman-like assurances of routine like the yellow school bus coming on time in the afternoon, the alarm clock's reliable beep every morning, *Arthur* switching to *PBS News Hour* my cue for dinner prep. When new factors forced me to change my navigation, these talisman-like markers marked a now-obsolete route.

When my daughter had asked how Aunt Cindy would know to come and get her, I wondered if not feeling well was psychosomatic, as the surgeon's nurses on the phone implied. They had responsibilities, too, long lists of patient calls to return. They'd say "everyone has pain," and I'd say "three weeks later and I have a fever," and they'd say "but not a high fever," also "so make an appointment." I had made an appointment ten days earlier, which required the afterschool sitter a second time that week, and I'd used one of my at-home days when I should have graded papers to drive into the city to the surgeon's.

If my daughter rode the bus in the afternoon I had forty more minutes to work; if I drove her to school in the morning I had forty more minutes to sleep. I drove her to school the next morning and, infused with caffeine, social reserve not yet operational, I spoke to someone else as if to myself. After delivering my daughter into the classroom, I walked to the parking lot beside a father I knew from village gatherings, our kids in slippery herds around us in Halloween costumes or bib tags for field day, clamoring about cupcakes, hot dogs. Most dads avoided me, single by choice. Mothers were curious. One said, "I have friends who are single mothers and they don't endanger their kids, but they're so busy they forget to turn on the old mental camcorder. They miss the fun."

As the pleasant dad and I unlocked our cars, I said, "I had a surgery almost a month ago and don't feel better." He got a look on his face like a good husband would get. I eventually had a good husband so that's how I know. But he wasn't my husband. We'd chatted as he dropped off and picked up kids because his job was nearby and his wife's wasn't. I was wearing a sweatsuit. It was a cold day, so I'd thrown on my warmest coat, fake-fur, knee-length. Paired with stylish but understated clothes, with my hair washed and makeup applied, it could be an interesting fashion statement. He looked at my face, my wild eyes. My hair was wild too. I know because a few seconds later I got in my car and flipped down the visor mirror. "Maybe talk to a doctor," he said, backing away.

I drove to the village doctor's.

I said to the receptionist, "The doctor referred me to have a surgery three weeks ago, and I never got well." She told me to sit down as other patients arrived. Then a nurse took me to a room and returned with the doctor who said he'd do a field test since lab test results wouldn't come back in time. He'd place a finger on each side of my cervix, deep to the lateral fornix with pressure towards the anterior abdomen, while using his other hand to apply external pressure to the pubic bones in the center of the pelvis while watching for the chandelier sign, as textbooks call it, wherein if the patient has a post-op infection she shrieks and reaches for an imaginary chandelier, he said, as I shrieked while reaching.

The nurse drew blood for a white blood cell count, which the doctor completed in his tiny onsite lab. He wrote a prescription for a broad-spectrum antibiotic. He said: "I know you're a single parent. Make childcare arrangements." He explained I'd come back for another test in the morning. If the count stayed the same or went up, he'd check me into a hospital in the city or college town. "If this infection is resistant, time is not on our side."

I called the big-hearted, sardonic sitter and asked, if need be, she could watch my daughter. I called the sitter I'd used a few years before, JoAnn, whose mother had died a good death, for a second layer of my daughter's safety net. Or third. I was first. JoAnn hadn't worked since her mother died but said to give her number to the other sitter in case the other sitter had a conflict. My next white blood cell count was lower. But, the nurse said, if over the weekend I had vertigo, a spike in fever, changes in vision, I'd go to ER. On Sunday, my daughter and I stood in line picking up breakfast tacos, and we saw this nurse again. She put her wrist on my forehead. "No fever. I figured. You look almost peppy."

Another problem I didn't foresee was that since my schedule required not just daycare but, once a week, nightcare, which isn't a thing, my nighttime sitters would be hard to find and unreliable because a job so intermittent is a sideline. I asked to switch this class to day but my supervisor, due to a blind spot or preternaturally rigid managerial style, said no. When I made the request over his head, he changed my schedule to make it harder.

Who can find a virtuous woman? Her price is beyond rubies. Proverbs 31:10. That's about a wife, though. At first, I'd found my sitter named JoAnn. I worked at home when I could, and when I couldn't, I left my daughter at JoAnn's, her house eight miles away, but I found a semishortcut, impassable in wet weather, from JoAnn's house to the college town, and my daughter was still a babe in arms, easy to carry. When she was one, I used Mother's Day Out to give JoAnn time off, JoAnn's Day Off. Mother's Day Out was also said to be good for the child's socialization. I still used JoAnn for night class. When my daughter was two and three, I used JoAnn a few days a week and for my night class.

JoAnn's caring was a low-key miracle that lasted until it didn't. True, she argued about giving my daughter one of her medications. It made her heart beat too fast, JoAnn felt. I took my daughter back to the specialist who said my daughter's heartrate was fine, that "some agitation is unavoidable," and "this medication is vital." JoAnn still said no she wasn't giving a baby speedy medicine through a plastic mask like a gas mask. One day a week, my daughter missed a dose, which the doctor okayed. He said: "I take it this is the grandma." JoAnn also noted my daughter's food allergies and cooked and pureed, reporting foods my daughter loved. My daughter loved JoAnn, calling out in baby patois: OJann!

But after JoAnn's mother died, JoAnn was bone-tired. People get this way after a hard stretch of weeks, months, years. Not during. So for one year—the year my daughter was four, before kindergarten, which I'd relied on to go to work, while using the bulimic sitter and her successor the sardonic sitter—I used a Baptist preschool, eighteen-mile round trip, thirty-six extra miles every day. For night class, I hired a graduate student who ended up having absenteeism and, to replace her, an undergraduate with stellar references who one day stopped coming. So I called JoAnn who finished out that semester, my night classes.

JoAnn said years later it had been hard to watch me make plans. Triggering, as we say now. She'd been a single mother. "I don't assume childcare will fall through," she said, "but it can." When it did, my week stalled, broken until fixed. JoAnn's parenthood hadn't had the presupervision mine did, the interviews with social workers and preadoption checklists creating false confidence, no stone unturned. I turned over stones for years.

One night during the year before kindergarten—so the year I used the Baptist preschool, before I fired the graduate student with absenteeism, not a firing offense yet, I'd so far decided, finding substitutes, asking her to please not cancel again—the phone rang, my new stepfather. My mother was in ICU. My experience with extended family didn't match the advice I got from the Baptist preschool workers. They weren't my friends, as one of them, not even a supervisor, said. She was a single mother who worked at the preschool to be near her son. "Don't be friendly," she advised in a tense, puzzling whisper.

But I'd told one childcare worker, who'd said I looked tired, that my mother was in ICU, and she'd told the others. Advice based on the advice-giver's circumstance materialized. For context, I recounted a condensed version of my circumstance. People said: Still! Go see her or you'll feel everlasting regret! The sitter I hadn't fired—I liked her but couldn't count on her—was close to her mother and told me she'd reserved cheap plane tickets for me, "bereavement fare," which was a thing then. I just had to confirm them.

My mother had been married less than a year, her third marriage. Her first to my alcoholic father had lasted twenty-odd years. Her second to an obscenely violent man lasted another twenty years. He was violent to everyone so I'd stopped visiting out of concern for my safety, though I remained concerned for hers, and, yes, I did advise her to leave him, but she never did. Then he died, lucky break, and she married an apparently pleasant man. When I met him and his grown children at the wedding, they seemed nice. Eight months later, I flew to see her in ICU because I hoped not to feel regret, and she died unexpectedly while I was on my way, while I was on a plane reading a book by Dave Eggers. As we planned her funeral, her husband and his grown children still seemed nice.

But I'd dithered before traveling because racing to and from Oregon with a four-year-old sounded hard. This decision was another fork in the road with optional routes into the future. Who would watch my daughter? The graduate student who'd so far canceled every other week wasn't good at routines, but she loved emergencies. She offered to stay overnight with my daughter one night. JoAnn took a few days. Two childcare workers from the Baptist preschool, younger than me, the age of aunts, each volunteered for an overnight. People passed my daughter around, dropped her off, picked her up.

The short trip to see my mother in ICU to preempt regret turned into ten days and nights, none of the nights with sleep for me. Even before I left, I hadn't slept, deciding stay, go, speculating how my mother's death at some far-off future point might be hard to process. The night before I traveled I didn't sleep, typical, not sleeping the night before travel, nor during, the unfamiliar bed, lights, noises. Choosing a coffin and burial clothes, writing a eulogy, delivering it, good manners by day, grief at night—my brain ran on high, making new neural paths to register that my mother, locus of love and regret, was dead.

I assumed a return to my bed, my neighbor's dusk-to-dawn yard light making familiar squares on my bedroom walls, would relax me. When I got home, a Baptist preschool worker said, "*Someone is glad to see you!*" My daughter's face was a mix of glee and terror. I put her to bed. I got into bed. I couldn't have slept forty minutes when she shook me awake. All night, all week, all month. Weeks into these multiple shakings-awake per night, I wasn't sleepy, just dull-witted and, once I bestirred myself, robotically coherent.

A Baptist preschool worker advised me to let my daughter sleep in my bed, but neither of us slept. I called JoAnn, who said to put a pallet in my room, show it to my daughter, and tell her if she went to bed in her room and woke she could move there only if she didn't wake me. I went to REI in the college town and bought a pallet. A year later, during kindergarten, she was still moving to the pallet—during the months I fell ill, during the lead-up to surgery, and afterward, the virulent post-op malaise. She grew too tall, so I went to town and bought a bigger pallet. I'd kiss her goodnight in her room, breathing deep the scent of child skin, and go to bed alone. I never woke until daytime's first placid minute. She'd have slipped across the house, to the pallet, under the quilt, to sleep.

I tried moving the pallet a few feet from my bed with the plan to bit-by-bit move it farther from my small room toward hers. But every morning, it was tucked back in the rectangular spot near my bed. She kept growing until, rolling over, she'd thump the closet and wake me. I explained this, and she offered to move to the hall outside my room and sleep there on a palliative pallet, thin layer on a hard, cold floor, harder and colder in the hall.

Quitting the pallet always registered as better sleep for both of us in a hypothetical future but a bad night right now, tonight. So I didn't. To be clear, pallet-reliance wasn't co-sleeping. Co-sleeping was when my daughter slept in a cradle next to my bed. Co-sleeping was when she was too big for the cradle and moved to a crib in her room, and a baby monitor amplified her small cries and I'd go feed her, falling asleep on her floor, my hand through the crib railing. Before my daughter arrived, a social worker described both bed-sharing and co-sleeping as good for bonding, though not everyone gets enough sleep while bed-sharing, she added. Co-sleeping, with the baby in your room in a playard, was easier. Playard? I'd asked her. Playard is another word for "playpen," archaic now, bad connotations. The social worker said, "You, if you fall in love, will want privacy." She pointed out that it would be tricky in a new relationship to have sex only during school or daycare.

When I first fell in love with my husband—rare, thrilling, physical encounters, and conversation about childcare that made encounters possible—we emailed. Texting wasn't a thing yet. I mostly nixed phone calls because, after putting my daughter to bed, I had chores. He had a cleaning service. He and his ex-wife lived near each other, with shared custody and dovetailed schedules. When his son was a baby, they'd had a nanny. One phone call to the agency will replace an unsuitable nanny, as when, for instance, a neighbor informed them their nanny smoked a cigarette in the yard as the baby napped. This couldn't have been a firing offense for me, I'd have reasoned, thinking that even nonsmokers step outside while a baby is napping. I expressed envy, then self-castigation about my peculiar, extemporized childcare, perfected plans forever foiled, and he added that he and his ex-wife lived in a city with more options and two salaries to pay for the options.

I once drove into the city to have a rare, thrilling, physical encounter there, at his house, and I paid the big-hearted, sardonic sitter, who had a daughter my daughter's age, for my daughter to spend the night. But this sitter was still disturbingly hard to wake. So sooner than planned, I was having the thrilling encounters always at my house and more frequently.

I'd put my daughter to bed, then go to bed with my new boyfriend, who so far seemed unobjectionable. Afterward, I'd open the door, unroll the pallet. "My daughter has separation anxiety since I made a trip to my mother's funeral," I explained, leaving out that years had passed. One night, as I unrolled the pallet, he said he was afraid of stepping on her when he got up in the night. I told him pallet-reliance was like a tide-you-over sleeping pill, easy to start and hellish to stop. I laughed wildly as I sometimes did when a mother in the village would critique my child maybe in order to check off a developmental milestone for hers, saying, "she's not walking!?" or "don't tell me she still *naps*!?"

He asked for my permission to propose a plan. The next morning, he got down on one knee and held my daughter's hand. "Is there a toy you really want?" For months, she'd asked for an expensive pretend-CD player that played pretend-CDs that came with it, four tinny, shouty children's songs. I objected. She had a real CD player with real CDs, I said. He shook his head no to me. To her, he said, "If you try to sleep one night in your room, I'll buy it." She slept all night in her room the first try. She liked this better, she said in the morning, better than the floor. My boyfriend and I sipped coffee. My daughter put a pretend-CD in a plastic box, as a song about a muffin man flooded the kitchen.

What the preadoption checklist missed:

- Many single parents have extended family or something like it.
- A job with vaunted "flextime" means improvised childcare.
- A village is a childcare desert.
- You can get so reliant on a schedule planned by the day, the hour, the minute, that a small tweak derails you, and you're bone-tired after, not during.

Postadoption, your adult daughter won't care one whit about your retrospective doubts, belated clarity as you realize years later that the entire plan, prechecked, checked, and doublechecked, was flawed, that every week wobbled on the verge of collapse like a house you'd built yourself out of odds and ends creaking and shaking and shuddering at every unexpected gust. She'll blink and say, "That's not how I remember it at all." And describe instead a garden you once planted, tiny carrots she pulled out too soon; how she followed you with a toy vacuum when you used the big one; something she calls Wine and Popsicle Night; the treehouse you built for her birthday, a serene porch high, high in branches.

Every weekday except night-class day, I'd wait in my car for my daughter's school bus and talk by phone to Aunt Cindy in Florida, her voice via the cell phone tower waves like the voice of a noninterventionist god, consoling but too far-off for material help. JoAnn's help was practical and nearby. Twenty years later, which is to say last week, she sent me this unexpected message by way of her boyfriend's social media "chat":

Debra, this is OJann. I had a dream at dawn about our girl. She lay in my arms. I enjoyed her so much, her sweet face. How precious she was to hold those years ago. When I had this same dream 5 years ago, I ran into her in a restaurant with her friends when I had an errand in the city that day! I'm not going out today so that won't repeat, but she is in my heart.

Five years earlier, my daughter had come home from a restaurant near her high school where she'd gone to eat. She'd heard JoAnn calling her name. They'd hugged hello, smiling.

After I got married and my daughter and I moved to the city, my commute to work was long but no longer spiraling and ever subject to change as it had been in the village, new byways always added, back when I'd be at work in midday and my body, conditioned to mapped blocks of time, shifted into palpable high-alert before I even saw the clock telling me that Mother's Day Out or the Baptist preschool or the elementary school was ending soon. I'd wrap up my class or meeting, thinking: get in the car and drive. On night-class day, I'd think: sitter, arrive! In the city, my husband picked up my daughter at onsite afterschool care, made dinner, then supervised her homework, getting harder.

A wayward sitter replaced. An illness correctly diagnosed. When my mother died, a distressing gap in childcare filled as I negotiated tangled schedules, conflicting phone messages. I strategized. I made snap decisions about the reliability of care and caring on offer. Stopgap expediency assembled out of shortages isn't everyone's experience. It was mine.

When the seventeen-year-old sitter one afternoon left my daughter alone on a hill, my neighbor the other neighbors called Crabby Old Man saw her and drove her back to school, and the principal called me to come quickly. I did, and then I knocked on this neighbor's door to thank him, and he said: "All on your own, are you?" I had sitters, I said. A few days later as I waited for her bus, he came outside and said he wished for my sake I was married so I'd have help. Then he smiled and said, "I guess you've thought of that."

I hadn't. Despite my penchant for planning to forestall all future glitches, which had turned into a game-like obsession—progress, then obstacles, near-failure, rapid reassessment, agile maneuver, voilà, home free—I'd never thought about a helpful husband because I couldn't problem-solve one into being, nor a life in which I wouldn't be overextended, a life in which more people than me would love and protect my daughter all day and night, no strings, no caveats, would boundlessly and unlimitedly love her as my husband does now. I was enough, timetabled, adaptive, assessing late-breaking threats, amending my latest plan, relief flooding as reward. I'd have continued to be enough. But future lucky windfalls are as unexpected as pitfalls, and I didn't have to be.

A Gendered History of My Hunger

Each time I'd quit or get fired, I'd stuff into the trash the detachable part of my uniform, the apron, ruffled and perky at my first job at The Topper Café, or later, at elite restaurants, a no-nonsense and starched-stiff linen apron encasing me from chest to knees. I'd do this at the restaurant as I walked out, or at a gas station on my way home, vowing never again to wait on people, never again to make groveling yet assured eye contact with the person most likely to pay the bill, back then a man, but not too much eye contact if he was with his wife or girlfriend who might interpret my eye contact as brazen and weigh in, nitpicking the quality of service, despoiling my tip. That exact despoiling never occurred, though other versions did. Once, I was spectacularly stiffed, a theatrics of stiffing.

At a table of twenty diners, a woman ordered the shellfish stew appetizer as an entrée. The menu also listed an entrée-sized version. In the flurry of preparing a big order, with each course precisely sequenced, the kitchen mistakenly prepared the big shellfish stew, prepared the entrée as entrée, though I'd written *shellfish stew appetizer as entrée* and shouted this while hanging the ticket. I laid the entrée-sized shellfish stew before her as I laid nineteen entrées before the nineteen other diners and told her she'd be charged only for the appetizer stew. Maybe she was dieting and didn't trust herself to eat just some. Or she wanted the experience of power and prerogative for just one night, no concessions.

She told me to take it back and bring the appetizer-size, made fresh, not part of this one moved to a smaller bowl, though I did suggest to the chef we do precisely that, and wait five minutes, pretend. Testy, he said that the stew would cool and reheating is impossible. He sent me back to her with the large bowl of scallops, oysters, mussels, shrimp, and leeks in a creamy white wine and tarragon broth, and I'd have liked some, having smelled it near my head on a tray above my shoulders for weeks. With the entrée-sized shellfish stew still on my tray, I said the chef would make an appetizer-sized shellfish stew that would arrive in ten minutes. Meanwhile, her companions—the word means *ones with bread*, ones you eat with—were scarfing down lamb noisette and beef medallions.

I craved the noisette drizzled in gin and juniper sauce in honor of the snowy days of winter, stuffed with breadcrumbs and velvety gorgonzola; I craved it daily. And I wanted the potatoes gratin served with it, bathed in a rich sauce, broiled until bubbling, golden.

I'd have liked the beef medallions but didn't quite daydream about them.

Waiters could eat half-price from the sandwich menu served in the bar. But the profit margin on the dinner menu was so slim that if we wanted food from the restaurant at the bottom of the grand staircase in the Peery Hotel, registered as a landmark, we were customers.

The woman with the shellfish stew problem clamped her mouth into a line and said to take the shellfish stew of whatever-size off the bill because she was having just wine, so bring more wine now. I avoided her eyes as the rest of the diners ate with gusto, because she was furious. I set the bill down, around $600 even then because the others had ordered appetizers and entrées, bottles and bottles of wine, desserts, and coffees. A 15 percent tip would have bought my groceries for over a month—legumes, macaroni, cheap meat. She lunged for it, glasses on the table wobbling and clinking. Her companions said *oh my, so generous*, though a few looked my way in sympathy and searched their wallets and purses in vain for cash, understanding that the woman who was now rushing them out the door had paid a $600 bill to get access to the blank for my tip: $0.00.

When the headwaiter had assigned me the twenty-top table in lieu of several two-tops, three-tops, and four-tops, I'd been pleased. Diners at big tables often grow fond of the waiter, admiring her multitasking and considerate skill, her anticipation of their rhythm of want. Sometimes they asked my name, what I was studying in graduate school, tipping generously at the end because by then they're buzzed, sated, and feeling—even if this is a fleet illusion—rich. Ordering their first choice from a menu of pure poetry at what the *Salt Lake Tribune* restaurant critic called the best restaurant in the state, though I concede that the state was Utah, they've had one of the best experiences that money can buy.

Someone takes note, arrives with your heart's desire unveiled as opulently arrayed platters and sparkling goblets of jewel-toned pools. You have eaten and drunk like royal personages.

So far I'd eaten at the Peery Café just once with my boyfriend. I'd had trouble deciding what to order, for weeks in advance considering each menu item's potential mix of flavor. Without pleasure, I placed my order, one shot at gratification, promising myself I'd someday have more food, more money. Not long afterward, working while preparing to get married because I was accidentally three months pregnant, and my boyfriend, Chet, had gone and lost his job again, I turned to Keri, studying theater, and every waiter was studying theater, art, literature, anthropology, nothing apt to be remunerative without extreme talent, work ethic, versatility, flukes of fortune, and I said how stressful it was that Chet had lost his job. Keri said something like, "Nothing more stressful than that." And I said: "You know what I mind most? That we can't go out to eat for the foreseeable future."

We stared at the royal personages cutting, chewing, sipping.

Even Keri—we were all food snobs—scolded me and said to put myself in Chet's shoes, the poor man so worried about money with a baby on the way and me wanting fine dining.

It wasn't her fault she didn't know Chet never worried about money.

My far-fetched career was discussible. Next quarter, I'd take this or that class. Next year, I'd take this or that qualifying exam—advanced proficiency in a foreign language, four days of essay exams on a reading list of 280 items. When my exams were over, I'd finish writing my dissertation and scour national lists and hit the job market with blind faith. I'd say this aloud to myself while working. Other waiters did it too, our oral versions of academic planning calendars, our completion-vows made public. But about my private life I said to myself and others only what I was doing tomorrow or during the next few months. Because I knew the whole project, my relationship with Chet, was a nonstarter that had nonetheless started. And now I was saying in public what I was doing weeks from now, my wedding, and months from now, moving my computer into the cloakroom at home so the room where I studied could become a bedroom for the unborn baby.

I didn't lack fine dining.

I lacked signs of progress toward career aspirations that, even before this detour into unplanned pregnancy and marriage to the wrong person, felt unattainable because of institutional hurdles that, at the time, seemed as fixed as geological impasses. I'd mistaken one moment in history, the 1980s, for life. I was managing life according to what I could see, outlines and omens. I was managing life with high hopes while—as adages ever advise—tamping down hopes. Because none of us gets what we want. Not exactly.

I'd worked at two other restaurants in the city, first at a fine dining café that served both lunch and dinner. I was assigned to lunch though I'd requested dinner. I needed days free. I taught undergraduate classes, took graduate classes, graded papers, wrote papers and, long-term, my dissertation. Working lunches, a three-hour shift in the middle of the day, was too hard. But I was assigned to lunch; women just were. Men got dinner.

I didn't understand until years later when I saw a documentary about the ERA's doomed progress in the 1980s. Most expensive restaurants assigned women to lunches because dinner costs more than lunch, and alcohol is consumed, all of which drives up the bills and therefore the tips. Some expensive restaurants openly stated they didn't hire women for dinners, but most quietly did not. This practice began centuries earlier as a way of saving the best tips for men, who, by consensus, had families to support. By tradition, male waiters making themselves servile denoted luxury. People paid more for that.

I didn't fully understand I was bucking tradition when an upscale restaurant advertised for dinner waiters and I applied. The waiting-tables-only resumé I'd created was a work of art. It wasn't fiction. But the story I made it tell was crafted—I was studying narratology, history and theory of the novel. The first restaurant I'd listed was Mack's Truckstop, owned by my father's drinking buddy. I'd barely worked there but including it proved I'd overcome lowly beginnings. Next, Topper Café. Next, Déjà Vu, Eau Claire, Wisconsin's most chic restaurant, waitresses in leotards and wraparound skirts. Next, a restaurant in the Ramada Inn in Kansas as I earned a master's degree. I left off jobs not in food service, also one as a cocktail waitress and another as a bartender at a bar frequented by gravel pit workers, unhelpful in the story of a young waiter destined for greatness.

I got called for an interview. Alaskan King Crab was spelled "Alasskan" on the specials-of-the-day chalkboard; the chef, who had a bad temper, also had dyslexia, a headwaiter with a kind face confided. This headwaiter praised my resumé, asked what I was studying in school, said the restaurant so far hadn't used women at night but the time for change was now, and I was well-spoken. He'd schedule me for lunches this week and then dinners next week, he said, to acclimate the chef who was, the headwaiter added, old school.

When the lunch waiters, all women, saw my name on the dinner schedule, they were angry. "I have long experience," I murmured. One of them said, "I have ten years' experience working lunches right here."

What did the men, the dinner waiters, think? One night, the head-waiter was absent, and he'd deputized one of them. The deputized head-waiter assigned me tables so physically distant—an eight-top on the patio, a six-top on the lowest tier, three four-tops in the main room—that I ran in and out, up and down. The male waiters began carrying out my food the second it was plated, before, at my speediest, I could get back to the kitchen. Then they complained about my ineptitude to the chef, who glowered. When the new schedule was posted, I wasn't on it. "You were the first one. I blame myself for being gone that night," the headwaiter said, shaking his head.

The Peery Café, egalitarian, let women serve dinner.

One night, I hung up a food order, and, as trained, cut slits in the crust of a small loaf of sourdough for diners at my table so the bread, possible to tear now, would stay moist. The knife was sharp, as the chef once warned, having seen me fail to curl back my fingers on one hand while cutting bread with the other. I was distracted while cutting, thinking that finishing my PhD and getting a job as the mother of an infant might be hard. Impossible? I hadn't conceded that. People say worry is pointless: Why vicariously endure what hasn't happened and might never? But worry is helpful. If you think about a problem until you're crazy with it, you stumble onto outlandish solutions that sometimes work. I cut my index finger. Blood spurted. A flap of flesh the size of an anchovy dangled.

The headwaiter sent me to the ER. Gilbert, a customer, would drive me. He was a lonely, well-dressed regular who ordered dinner from the expensive menu but ate at the bar while interacting with staff. One day, listening to talk between a few of us studying literature, Gilbert erupted into speech, saying he was a poet. I paused to see what he meant. He wrote poems that no one read? If you love good poetry, truly nothing is worse than bad poetry. The bartender, an English major, pressed for details. Gilbert hemmed, hawed, then said that he had a poem in the *New Yorker*. Someone said: wonderful, what issue? Gilbert said: oh, not out yet. "Forthcoming," I emended primly, arranging food on a tray. From then on, Gilbert's poem was forever forthcoming. Fantasies, by definition, are.

In the ER waiting room, a nurse assumed Gilbert was my husband. I corrected her. I can't remember why I didn't call my husband-to-be. He was watching a rented movie due back the next day? I was bleeding out too fast? A doctor sewed the flap back on.

On Valentine's Day, the busiest night of the year, I was relieved to have taken the bandage off. I inspected my newly healed scar, a pink seam. I'd work better without the bandage and Latex cot, a finger condom that keeps wounds away from customers' food. I needed money for medical bills because by now I was having a miscarriage. A few days earlier, I'd told Keri: "I'm distracted." She'd noticed, she said. Everyone at work knew about my incomplete miscarriage and low-grade contractions. The OB-GYN was waiting for big contractions to kick in, but we couldn't wait forever. A nonviable pregnancy turns septic. My boyfriend was still out of work. Keri and other waiters didn't mind that I was spacy, but the chef, she warned me, was still mad I'd cut myself. He talked about firing me.

I worked too fast that night. While cutting bread, I again lost control of the knife. I again sliced off the same slab of finger. Because the restaurant was busy, I made the snap decision to wrap my hand in a white linen napkin, which I tossed off for a fresh one every few minutes. I hid my hand wrapped in blood-soaked linen as well as I could, striding through the dining room with a tray hoisted over my head. Bloody hand tucked behind my back, I slid plates in front of diners. With couples arriving in twos, fours, sixes, eights, the staff working at capacity, not to mention dim lighting and plentiful au jus the color of blood, no one knew I'd cut myself again until the chef left to smoke a cigarette and I peeled back the grisly napkin. Keri sneaked me out the door to Gilbert's car. The ER doctor, alarmed at data the triage nurse had recorded, gave me pills to induce contractions.

———

I first developed a yearning for never-before-tasted foods while reading books when I was a child. I read Book of the Month Club books delivered to my mother and thrillers my dad bought. He also bid on boxes of books at auctions, ancient bestsellers with brittle pages. Once, when I was ten, I told a waiter I wanted lobster tail. My father and mother had ordered steak, my siblings burgers. My mother objected: the price. She'd never had lobster, no desire! I'd read about lobster in an old volume of F. Scott Fitzgerald stories.

In stories by the British writer H. H. Munro, in *Love Story* by Erich Segal, in *Three O' Clock Dinner* by Josephine Pinckney, in *The Sunlit Ambush* by Mark Derby, in *Mrs. Miniver* by Jan Struther, I read about foods I didn't know. I pored over my mother's wedding present, *The Betty Crocker Picture Cookbook*, sections on how to host with a maid, how to a have a buffet in the rumpus room, why we serve savories with cocktails. One day, I removed a soufflé from the oven and gave some to my brother. "What's *in* it?" he said. My mother encouraged this cooking, to a point. When I asked for a rump roast and gingersnaps to make sauerbraten, she said to make a pot roast instead. I added coffee because I'd read that tip in the newspaper and, thinking about gingersnaps, molasses. I noticed, and not for the last time, that cooking is wishing and eating is less exciting than wishing.

My slow miscarriage was low-level pain as I rushed between school and work, followed by a final late-night volley of pain. Canceling the wedding was a good idea I rejected as awkward. I'd invited my family. Chet had invited his. I'd told classmates I was getting married. I'd told my dissertation director too, while I was rescheduling my comprehensive exams for before the baby's due date, saying, no, that's right, I was not married but would be before the baby arrived. Not that being unmarried or unmarried once the baby arrived should have mattered for my future scholarships or letters of recommendation, my mind-boggling career going forward. But being uncontroversial probably did. Did I tell Chet, whom elsewhere in my oeuvre I've called "volatile," that I didn't want to marry him since I'd had a miscarriage, due to either natural causes or the gut punch Chet threw one night? I broached the subject, looked at his face, and dropped it.

My dad said as he got off the plane that everyone had come a long way and he hoped the wedding wouldn't be sad. The owner of the Peery Café, not to be confused with the chef, had heard from Keri that I'd worked straight through a long miscarriage, also about my upcoming nuptials he saw as one of life's great moments made poignant due to my miscarriage. "Ah, poor kid," he'd said. He offered me a wedding feast at cost. He created the restaurant's menus and shared my passion for the way words and food blend to make desire tangible yet mystical. He once heard me answer a diner's query about the winter slaw served with duck breast. "Red cabbage, garlic, lemon, balsamic vinegar. It's more than the sum of its parts, it . . . it tastes how I imagine the color purple must taste." The owner later said, "You never want to overdo it. Nevertheless, that was appealing."

Our table was a seven-top: the bridal couple, my sister, Chet's parents, my father and stepmother. I ate lamb noisette and sipped a complex white burgundy gleaming like topaz. My sister whispered that I looked tired. My father rambled, rehashing arguments he'd had with people no one knew. Chet's parents had been poor, but Chet's stepfather, via education and hard work, and Chet's mother, via marriage, had scraped into the illusion of the upper-middle-class, though they declared bankruptcy a few years later. Chet told me later his mother took him aside that night to say our marriage was doomed because my eyes looked sad, either due to the miscarriage or because I'd been raised by a drunk.

So I didn't cancel my wedding because telling family members to take a hit on plane tickets while I left Chet, which meant renting a new apartment without money, was a daunting midsemester to-do list. I needed a savings account, not to mention an era that hadn't arrived, one in which a woman who'd entered a relationship that became abusive—a succinct term not yet in use—could leave him without a blow-by-blow explanation. I also felt confused about canceling with the officiating judge and what to do with the $100 dress. I fixed on minor setbacks that, in better moments, I'd have vaulted past.

Six weeks after I got married, a professor had offered money from the department slush fund to any graduate student who'd host a reception for a visiting writer, and I'd volunteered. I sat on my couch watching people mill, snack, sip. I felt plateaued. After studying at increased speed because I'd planned to take my comprehensive exams months early, I rescheduled them at the usual time, a year away. Chet had a job for now. Trees sprouted green. I exceled at making savory appetizers. Chet owned a barbeque smoker and liked making meat for my classmates, almost all of them men, who slapped his back. I watched them across the room, gnawing ribs. Did I mention I was sad? A miscarriage is sad.

The guest-of-honor left, and a woman classmate sat down next to me. Women students were uniformly good. None would have been admitted without stellar portfolios because admission committee members were men born in the 1940s and, like every reader, less likely to value work about themes that didn't reflect their experiences. Bias is unconscious, or its extent is. I can't speak for the other six women out of thirty PhD candidates, but I felt provisionally admired. *A rare woman who thinks and writes like a man*, a professor said, a compliment. We couldn't change that. So we surveilled each other.

I can't duplicate the exact logic of what my woman classmate said to me that day. She maybe thought a miscarriage was like a bad period and mine was over. She said I probably didn't see how my decisions and "labile insecurity"—I still remember that—affected her, a woman who'd come in on a better scholarship than me the same year I'd come in. I hadn't known about her better scholarship until she said this. She mentioned it to emphasize pressure she felt, she said. More than me, she said, she, "golden girl," felt scrutiny.

The word "sexism" didn't yet describe institutional privilege. Sexism so far meant a man making sexual overtures a woman didn't want. And some women did want, the man could always say back. Two women students at the party had slept with my dissertation director. One would marry him within the year, his second student-wife. Sexism didn't yet mean unconscious disregard for a woman's talent or skill. In the fifty-member department where I was getting my degree, two women professors taught classes that hadn't fit my degree plan. So I'd never studied with a woman. Before the party, I'd dressed female-but-not-sexy, ruffled-yet-tailored. Now the sunset was orange in the window. I focused on not crying—not crying about what, though?—until the party was over.

I finished the degree and moved to the other side of the country, with Chet as my "faculty spouse," new coinage. This was the year Clarence Thomas was confirmed as Supreme Court justice, people talking about whether to believe Anita Hill. I rode in on one of the 1990s waves of hiring women quickly: making up for lost time. Three of us arrived in my department that year. I couldn't tell my male colleagues apart except for differences in how they said hello: nervous but kindly, nervous but aloof, kindly but leering. Chet stayed unemployed. We stayed broke. We ate legumes, macaroni, cheap meat.

I left Chet by getting a new job in a new state, which turned out to be Texas. I took up with a nice enough local. He noticed I'd never had enough of what I wanted. He took me to a restaurant with prices so high they weren't on the menu; another restaurant people flew to in private planes; another with peacocks in the yard and chilled shrimp on the table atop butter lettuce with vine-ripened tomatoes and dressing made with secret ingredients, including gentlemen's relish and sieved hard-boiled egg yolks. I couldn't afford this. The man pretended he could. When we broke up, I helped pay down his credit card.

For fifteen years, I lived in the country, an hour's drive from the city where most of my friends lived. Single, I bought a house. Single, I became a mother. Single, I felt my friends should be rewarded for driving to visit me. Let's say, it was winter. I'd make a layered appetizer, pickled herring, apple slices, mustard, capers, onions, sour cream, to be eaten on wheat crackers while sipping cold vodka. Next, a pork loin roasted with dried apricots, also potatoes gratin, broiled until bubbling golden. Summer, pasta with tomatoes, basil, and brie, or maybe chicken with olives and figs. Fall? Beef medallions with winter slaw that tastes like the color purple. Or seafood stew with creamy wine and tarragon broth.

My cravings stopped. One night at a restaurant in the city, I sat between my daughter, who was still young, and my husband, who was still a promising boyfriend then. Like me, he'd scraped his way forward via education and hard work. Like me, he had a stable job, home equity, a child. That night was my birthday, also my friend's birthday. Some years, we can't celebrate together because her career takes her to Lisbon, Paris, Dublin. But this year, we did, with another friend, a woman writing her dissertation about mid-twentieth-century women writers. She arrived carrying gaudy flowers—one bundle for me, the other for my friend. My residual worries about money, gone. My residual tension about elbowing my way into a profession slow to let us in, gone. The fear that one of us, token woman, symbolic hire, would get the one spot, or one of a few spots, gone.

Someone held up a glass filled with ruby or topaz to make a toast and my daughter told the waiter: "I'll have the artichoke appetizer as an entrée." The waiter told her that most kids just order plain pasta. She shook her head because she likes artichokes. We all laughed, gladioli heaped in the middle of white linen, our laughter rising. For a moment, we seemed to rise. But the dining room was filled with many royal personages. The next morning, my husband—new boyfriend then—said we'd perhaps laughed so loud and often we'd maybe ruined the illusion for other royal personages. Then we looked at the bill everyone had kicked in on. Due to tipsy oversight and the now-standard practice of levying a tip on big tables, we'd tipped 40 percent. I don't even remember eating. The food was fine.

2

Something New to Say about
Domestic Violence

When I started writing, I wrote fiction and people asked how much was true. They asked bluntly or subtly if events in my books had happened to me. The every-person's harrowing memoir wasn't a genre yet. Memoirs were still something former celebrities wrote. Readers assume, not incorrectly, that inspiration is at least partly autobiographical. I'd deflect questions with a sound bite about the power and necessity of imagination. "Invented stories create order we want but can't find in the chaos of life," I'd say. This is true but off-topic because a story that's artful can also be autobiographical. Yet high-flown talk about art made people happy, and they'd stop thinking about my life and think instead about art versus life, realism versus reality. Realism is not reality. Realism is using craft to simplify reality, to make it "relatable," as people like to say when realism succeeds.

To be clear, an editor once asked me for revisions because the protagonist's stepfather's rage seemed unrealistic; another wanted revisions on another book because this time the protagonist's ex-husband's rage seemed unrealistic. I revised to make these secondary characters occasionally neutral or vulnerable and give them backstory, bad childhoods.

To be clearer, I was teaching when a student handed in a story with a mother's abusive boyfriend in it, and her classmates asked her to "humanize" him because he seemed like a one-dimensional stereotype. She looked alarmed. Her next draft included moments when he was sedentary as well as aggressive, also a new scene rich with detail—a timer going off as Pillsbury cookies baked too long in the oven, neighbor kids' trikes rolling past outside the window as the boyfriend left the louvred bedroom door open and raped the protagonist's mother as the protagonist watched. No one in the class spoke. "Maybe foreshadowing and backstory and causality won't cover every effect," I said. "Maybe some characters get written like once-in-a-lifetime bad weather no one saw coming."

When I was middle-aged, I sat with my new husband I'd married after fifteen single years. Marrying him turned out to be one of my good decisions. We were with his ex-wife, and I already liked her, and, years later, I love her like a relative, a good one. We were at a first meeting with a family therapist, in search of insight about coparenting. This therapist wasn't for us, we quickly decided. Too bellicose, my husband's ex-wife said. I hadn't been paying close attention because I'd been staring at a book on a shelf behind him, its title about how women contribute to violence happening to them and can learn to stop.

I've written fiction that, at times, depicts domestic violence. I've fielded questions about it as journalists try to make an author interview edgy. I've researched it. I went to therapy in its aftermath and sometimes knew more about it than the therapists in my coverage plan.

Men who are victims hesitate to get help because resources are for women, yes. My friend protected himself by contacting a battered women's shelter. Violence can be mutual, yes. A couple I knew in school had to be pulled apart on the courthouse lawn at someone else's wedding. Violence occurs in same-sex relationships, yes. Writing what she cares about, a friend wrote about a woman and her unnamed lover, an ominous "she" whose presence infused the air, dripped from the walls, blew the roof off. I found this story so relatable that when I talked to my friend about it I slipped up and called the lover "he."

But the violent partner is usually male and the recipient female, maybe due to engrained gender roles emphasizing male power and female compliance, and the person with more upper-body strength, usually male, is undeterred by fear. Domestic violence occurs in every social class. I've read this but know, firsthand, that it happened to me and to my mother as we tried to stay in the middle-class, while the inflicting men were going bankrupt.

When I moved to my first professional job, my then-husband was going bankrupt for a second time. The first time was before we'd met. Wanting to avoid too-personal conversations with people I didn't know well, I took to saying, and he took to believing, that he'd moved for my career and therefore his career had suffered. He'd never had one, but I needed an explanation for why he didn't have a job and I did, why activities and outings a potential friend suggested were off the table. My discretionary income was nil. My nondiscretionary income was scant: money for current bills, also outstanding bills he'd had before we'd met, but he hadn't told me. A person to whom I rationalized my then-husband's unemployment was my houseguest, a woman I'd met at a writers conference.

The weeklong conference at which the woman and I led workshops had been a reprieve from worries about money; worries about my new job teaching graduate students, some receptive, others offended that I, the same age or younger, had turned out to be the teacher; and worries about my then-husband's anger. Worries about money were ongoing. Worries about my job were new. Worries about my then-husband's anger were atmospheric. Living with it was like living in high humidity with the threat of storms. I'd long ago learned to work, keep house, choose clothes and style my hair in this climate. When he erupted, I battened down.

The woman was scheduled to come to my city for a book signing. By then, we were pen pals, amusing each other with nineteenth-century letter-writing tropes. "Dear Bosom Friend," one of our letters might start. She'd describe a date she'd been on, as per Chekhov: "I went to the town of S_____." These letters were my social life. If new neighbors or colleagues invited my then-husband and me over, he strained to make conversation and came home testy, and we'd have had drinks. Preconditions. People didn't ask us a second time. We didn't ask them back, avoiding stress and expense. But I impulsively invited the woman to sleep on the floor in my study, sure she'd opt for a hotel.

She said yes, and we went to her book signing, then sightseeing and window-shopping. In the kitchen—next to my study, where she was re-arranging her suitcase—I was wiping down the stove after cooking dinner. My then-husband stood near, asking me to try harder to do as he'd asked. Exactly what I can't remember. Cleaning. Cooking. Avoiding window-shopping so I'd avoid wanting money. But I felt lighthearted, like I was away from home, not in it. When the houseguest arrived, she'd made friendly small talk with my then-husband about baseball. In the years since I'd tumbled into a life with him and didn't find a way out, I'd learned he wasn't used to people taking time to talk to him.

Half-facetious, or years-furious, I whispered: "If I don't? You can't hit me right now."

He turned a dark shade of red and left the kitchen.

In books of fiction, I've written detailed scenes depicting the tense lead-up, serial blows, the husband knocking the protagonist down and kicking her while wearing boots, or maybe ramming her head into the bedroom wall, and the house was old, and the plaster cracked, expos-ing old-fashioned lath. The next day, still mad, knowing he was calm on days after, even contrite, she didn't get out spackle and paint. She got a black marker and drew a circle around the hole, and the wall stayed that way for weeks, like décor. She'd forgotten about it by the time a classmate stopped to borrow a book, asked to use the bathroom you got to by pass-ing through the bedroom, came back, and said: "What's up with the hole circled with marker?" The protagonist said, "The wall got damaged when we moved furniture. The circle is a reminder to repair it." The classmate shrugged, as in: weird but whatever.

OK, I didn't use that in a previous book.

Realism is detailed scenes, but not too many with the same theme, monotony, bad pacing.

I wrote more scenes about dailiness. Normalcy in between is real. It's also realism: a necessary break for readers. But a few vivid scenes help readers sense that the protagonist felt white-light-electrified until it was over, relieved after it was, and then behind at work and too distracted to decipher how she got here or how to get out. At one of those book clubs to which authors get invited, a reader might volunteer that the violence wasn't vivid enough, so obviously made up. Another will say the violence seemed true, but the protagonist could have saved herself sooner. What the second book club lady meant was that violence would never have happened to her, and she's probably right.

I've long since lost touch with the houseguest, but after her visit, I told her by phone—my then-husband in another room, door closed—that I was mad he didn't look for a job, mad about his moods, mad about paying bills. Personality traits I tried to showcase were my gumption, which is also recklessness, and my optimism, AKA Pollyanna syndrome. She said, "Move. See where pieces land. Get a different job." This seemed like an indirect solution. But I knew how to apply for jobs, pack, rent a U-Haul. I moved across country, planning to bring my then-husband but, due to misunderstandings I never clarified, I left him. I called her when I was living alone. "Our fights got physical," I said, sidling up to my first-time revelation. Not counting a time, early on, I'd carelessly let on, sad fallout. The houseguest knew, she said: "That time you were in the kitchen. I heard."

I could have seen the violence coming if I'd been a god-like author of my life and not a character in it, with limited perspective, low visibility, ambient pressures like fog. For backstory, the furthest I can get is my grandparents. If records had been kept, I'm sure the story goes further, infinite regress: generations of anger and bewildered adaptation. One grandmother hit sons with wire hangers and skillets but not all the time, only during low troughs, mental illness. A grandfather used a leather strap, not unusual then.

My parents used to hug and kiss each other while their little children looked on, lingering kisses and full-body embraces at their supper-hour reunion after eight hours apart, separate workdays. I heard a muted argument late at night, once. When I was older, he drank and ran around town and neighboring towns, and she tried to keep up. Once, he came back by himself, leaving her alone in some Podunk place. Once, she came back by herself, walking eight miles from a country tavern, or she started, and someone saw her and gave her a ride. He met a woman, his chiropractor's secretary. He wanted out. My mother didn't like him anymore. But she loved him. She was ripe for the picking and got picked.

I was an adult when she married the violent man, and here's his humanizing detail: he thought Cyndi Lauper singing "Time after Time" was the Vienna Boys Choir singing a Christmas song. Endearing if anything else about him had been. He never hit me, but only because I locked doors, the house quaking. The next day, I left and stopped returning.

But even before she married him, I had a faulty bad-vibes sensor. Everyone in my family did. We picked up everything and nothing. Ignoring false warnings, we missed real ones. We were also quick to feel affection, quick to feel hurt, quick to shift between love and lashing out, a balmy moment, then a squall or hard freeze. Occasionally, my dad swung at me. I had my pet words, my perfected sentences in which to deliver them, and I'd practice in my head until I'd spill one, then see his raised arm and jump. My mother, in extremis, and only when I was a hyped-up teenager, hit *at* me, frantic parenting. But a parent is scared when a kid old enough to leave home alone is on the cusp of unsafe decisions. I was on the cusp often, and no one parents well while scared. Her voice like a siren, arms waving, or a yardstick or vacuum cleaner extension waving, she flailed at me, her fear.

Women Who Love Too Much was a bestseller in 1985, but I read it in the 1990s, and by then, I was living alone again except for an outside dog, a coonhound. He bit the veterinarian. I signed him up for dog obedience class, and he bit the instructor, who returned my fee, saying the dog's problems were my fault because I'd taken for a pet a dog from a breed about which I knew squat. The dog mellowed after a rattlesnake bit him, and I nursed him back to health, noting his tender heart beneath the bluster. I retrained myself to think my former husband's failings weren't my fault. Women Who Love Dogs Too Much, I thought, sorting it all out. A dog that flunks obedience class is *unsocialized*.

An abusive spouse is *uncivilized*. A police officer had once said this to my then-husband, while shining a flashlight into my bloody mouth. No I didn't press charges. I'd barely dialed 911. We lived across the street from the director of Graduate Studies, who, I was glad to discover, never woke to see cop cars and swirling red lights. A woman I know now, in this decade, didn't get tenure after telling colleagues about her abuse. She said: "Would you have?" I didn't say—she felt too bad—but no. Standards for promotion are objective. Interpretation of whether they're met aren't always. The least humane committee member is the group-dynamic bully. For every colleague who cares, another sees you as unstable. The police officer said, "Everyone gets mad at his wife. But this is uncivilized."

Odd that I kept my life-wide secret for five years. Because I usually offer up my mistakes, signaling to others that I'm no threat: no hostility or aggression required. For five years, I didn't find a way out. My mother didn't leave her husband due to what's termed "financial abuse." She got persuaded to put her retirement savings into his failing business, then had to stay and run it. I took out loans to pay down my then-husband's debts. Before that, when I first moved in with him, I'd drained my bank account. But I was a graduate student. I'd always depleted funds while moving: deposit, first and last month's rent.

He hit me as soon as I didn't have an apartment of my own. He wasn't careful yet, as he later was, to land blows where they don't show, which was my torso, covered by clothes, the sides and back of my head, covered by hair. All these years later, if I bump my head while cleaning or maybe gardening, and afterward I gingerly touch it, assess its soreness, I'm in time-travel. After that first fight, I wasn't careful yet either. I was going hiking with my friend, and I had on a tank top, and she saw the finger-bruises encircling the hand-bruises, my arm. She said I should stay with her a few days as I called my parents to get money and then I'd move out. My dad's money was tied up, new household, new business, new wife. He was also likely to yell he couldn't fix a problem I'd made. I'd have needed to cancel my lease. Women's shelters were new concepts then, providing beds, not legal counsel.

"Then I can't be your friend," she said. She meant this as my incentive, I guess. I couldn't leave. She thought I wouldn't. I still don't know why she needed to keep her distance, what she saw in my life that reverberated through hers, but it must have been daunting. I'd see her in class, after class, at a bookstore. I'd arrange my face: shy, welcoming, confident, empty of expectation. I tried on many expressions. She turned away.

Domestic violence wasn't the premise of fiction I wrote, but it was context. I wrote scenes, first drafts always sensationalistic overkill, but revision works like toner, minimizing harsh notes. In life, I'd sometimes lift this part of my past out of the bin of secrets. In life, people want concise terminology, not scenes. I was at a meeting where a hothead objected to policy changes, and he yelled—specks of spit spraying, face red—and pounded the table. Afterward, a nice colleague smiled at me, then rolled his eyes in dismay. I was tenured, so I said I'd felt the same, adding that I'd had the impulse to leave the room but had forced myself to stay in my chair. Not the same, I realized. The nice colleague looked confused. I said, "Reverse-Pavlovian response. I used to be in a violent marriage."

By the time I sat with my new husband and his ex-wife in a family therapist's office, I felt I'd set the subject aside. I don't remember the therapist's name, only his cropped mustache, his talk about "tough love," the book on a shelf behind his head with its title about women contributing to violence. When I found it on a website for out-of-print books, I saw that the therapist was its author. I can't find it online now, nor the therapist who's since moved or retired. Though the therapist's bio for his practice hadn't mentioned men's rights, his author bio did. People sometimes confuse men's rights with men's liberation, that 1970s movement in which men object to machismo. But men's rights is antifeminist, pro-machismo. The book's point was that women should control their tone, word choice, gestures.

When I'd held still, stayed quiet, the episodes ended more quickly, true. But sometimes I was mad every difference of opinion got settled unfairly and hit back, not for long, the retaliation. In a midzone of self-control, I objected in a "shrill" voice. I might, to use a phrase from the book written by the therapist, "weaponize home furnishings." I'd decide a vase or saucer was nonessential and hurl it. As beatings grew routine, they got worse, as did my self-control. Years later, while reading the book's synopsis on the used-books website, I tried to see its strategy working and came up with an analogy that fell apart, an S&M safe-word: both partners don't want the bad level, the abuser has power, the abused's tone is a safe-signal. . .

When I met my now-husband, we began to collaborate on decisions, open to each other's caveats and fine points. I assumed we'd one day disagree about a big problem, but no. Yet once we were in the same house, managing two careers, two children's schedules, and my husband managed care for his parents, we started having those trivial fights like comedy skits, hyperbolic characters and mishaps, then the wrap-up in which everyone is chuckling and mutually abashed. A fault-line opened between us: different conceptions of comedy.

Either that or we passionately disagreed about mustard.

Or when to carry a chest of drawers to the alley.

The mustard dispute occurred as I was cooking a holiday meal, guests soon to arrive, kids with their questions about have you seen my this or that, and I told my husband we had yellow mustard but needed brown.

He misunderstood, went to the store, and bought yellow. I needed brown to keep cooking. When the kids come for visits now, bringing their partners, recalling childhood, the mustard dispute is legendary. They'd watched from the porch. My husband had followed me to my car, leaning into my door. Me: I can't do anything without the mustard. Him: I'll go. For the kids, this was far-off pantomime. I put the car in reverse. I said: I'll feel calm getting the mustard, not waiting. I took my foot off the brake. The car rolled. He jumped, saying: You want to run me over! I said: I don't! The kids' version: OMG, our parents' worst fight was who buys mustard faster.

The furniture dispute occurred when I was fresh from a shower, lotion still on my hands. I'd said: I'll help you move that chest of drawers after work. I was thinking about my lecture, my students, my commute. I'd said this twice. He said: It will take only a minute. The drawers slid. The chest wobbled. We got it downstairs and outside in humid air. My hands, greasy, sweating, lost hold, and the chest crashed in pieces on the pavement. I went inside, and I slapped the door shut. He'd say slammed. He was a few feet behind me. He'd say inches. I had a bad temper, he said. Haughty, I answered, "You've led a sheltered life." He said to lower my voice. I thought he meant volume. "I'm not yelling," I hissed. "The pitch," he said. Close-up and histrionically basso profundo, I said: "I'm not yelling."

A day later, he paused, made wary eye contact, told me what he was about to say wasn't justification for "guys with short fuses, your exes," but my hostile body language and rapid-fire articulation, "like Katherine Hepburn on steroids," was provoking. I got mad all over again, yelling at him that now he'd mastered the men's rights angle, that book by the retrogressive therapist telling women to keep the peace with pleasant tones and gestures. "Deciding how to act based on how strong you aren't isn't a calculation men make, or not much," I said. He said a calculation he'd start making was how well he'd listened and what he didn't yet fathom. He'd try. Would I, please? So minor disagreements wouldn't escalate.

He used the plural, "guys with short fuses, your exes," because, when we'd first met, we'd told each other our lives. I'd used the phrase "abusive marriage." But we were falling in love, and he wanted to understand. I knew how to describe domestic violence in realism and reality, in novels and in casual conversation, vivid scenes versus bland descriptors, making it realistic or real, proving the protagonist or I could be believed, trusted. I paused, considering my answer. He asked: Did I grow up with violence? This was when people first started saying "rape culture" to encapsulate normalized low-grade violations, first rungs on a dangerous ladder. I said, "How and where I lived, people I knew . . . violence always seemed near and possible." I added I knew many people who'd been physically abused, that I'd had other relationships that got to a violent edge, not during the relationships, but as they'd ended.

Slowly, I began to use the advice from the retrogressive therapist's out-of-print book, or a summary of it on a used-books website. But only while arguing with civilized people I love now. I express myself during harried wrangles as carefully as I do talking over big decisions. At first, I playacted. I'd playacted calm at work. I could in marriage. And I'm a better parent for seeming deliberate and not-frantic as I love deeply while worried.

But congenial deportment wouldn't have stopped my then-husband's wreckage and rampage, cycles of pressure rising, falling, rising, then spent on me. He had a bad childhood, check; low self-esteem, check; no money, check; untreated clinical anxiety, probably. Domestic violence swept over me for five years because conditions were favorable. I didn't have financial assets. I grew up jumpy. I was transient, far from anyone to help. In the days after he'd hit, push, pummel, or slap me, or pull my hair, or worse, I'd notice that the body heals. It always healed. But my brain was harrowed, arranged into readiness for warnings that arrive so late I won't have time to prepare, into waiting while fortifying, my primitive reflexes roused, once useful vigilance outlasting use.

My Taciturn Valentine

My first date took me by snowmobile to a tavern that served minors. We didn't speak as the snowmobile roared through woods—we wore helmets, besides. In the tavern, we removed our helmets. But the jukebox throbbed loud polkas, and up and down the bar raucous elders traded insults. My exhilaration that night came from proximity, not conversation, the brand-new buzzing knowledge that the nearby body belonged with mine. Whether the strong, silent lover found in books and movies caused me to believe in the strong, silent lover sitting near me on a barstool, or the fantasy of the strong, silent lover sitting near me on a barstool—near any woman—causes his double to recur in art, is a chicken-or-egg question. Yet women fill silence well. They customize it. "Every night I give my body to my husband like a chalice," a woman wrote in a letter to Ann Landers I read as a schoolgirl, my interest piquing. As long as my boyfriend didn't talk, he was a void into which I poured thoughts so profound he apparently found them inexpressible.

Meanwhile, in the wilds of my youth, the language of hunting and fishing pervaded the discourse of love: *on the prowl*; *the one that got away*; *small fry*; *jailbait*; *she fell for him hook, line, and sinker*. It implied a distinction between predator and prey. Men were predators and women were prey, right? Everyone knows that a woman in hot pursuit makes a tactical error, but a man in hot pursuit is virile. And all around me, brute rivals seemed to await my boyfriend's inattention, so *strong* was a necessary attribute too.

One evening, the radio was tuned to a top-forty station five hundred miles away. Strange as it seems now, John Denver's song about his ex-wife sounded like poetry—reasonable poetry for a man who hunted and fished, I thought, eyeing my boyfriend. *Night in the forest. Mountains in springtime.* He could discuss these. Maybe they filled up his senses. But he couldn't make the next leap and equate bliss in the woods with bliss he felt spending time with me. Could I live the rest of my life never hearing words like these? A few days later, ironing my father's shirts, I decided I couldn't. I wanted to go to college. Did I go to college to find an eloquent lover? People have gone to college for less.

I moved to a small city, where one of my professors explained that when a male character in a nineteenth-century novel declares himself our satisfaction has been whetted by the long delay. True. Years of waiting for real boyfriends to say something reckless and extraordinary increased my thrill when Heathcliff erupted: "With all the powers of his puny being, he couldn't love as much in eighty years as I do in a day." If, by real life standards, a surly, obsessive suitor is stalker-material, in literature he's irresistible. I'm a professor now, and one semester, a student raced into my office, shut the door, told me she'd met Mr. Rochester. He hardly spoke, she said. His passion was unrelenting. They didn't want to be apart. I wondered how she knew this if he didn't speak. Perhaps she was thinking of the "real" Mr. Rochester, who told Jane Eyre not to leave or "the cord of communion will be snapt." I sent my warning in code. I emphasized the power inequity between Mr. Rochester and Jane, how Mr. Rochester's humbling at the end (blindness!) isn't feasible or even desirable. The student ignored me, a killjoy, and resumed her daydream.

But I understand. By the time I was in graduate school, I dreamed at night about John Donne. He looked like he does in the portrait for which he posed naked except for his shroud, also like the professor who read John Donne's poems aloud in class. Did John Donne speak in my dreams? Not often, but it was worth the wait: at first, smart, sexy analogies; as we grew closer, passionate avowals; later, unflinching spiritual insight. John Donne was the total package. A gap developed between my ideal and the men I met. One night, I kissed a classmate because he said Robert Coover's work was an assault on cliché-ridden templates society imposes on us. He wore a toupee that didn't quite match his remaining hair—this was before balding men shaved their entire heads to reveal, voila, the phallic head—and I felt if he'd quit wearing the toupee he'd not only look better but people would stop joking about it behind his back. Kissing, I'd tilt this way and that, obliging him to tilt, hoping the swaying would cause him to fling off the toupee and say something ardent about kissing as an assault on cliché-ridden whatever. He never unveiled his head nor his innermost self, though I'm sure some woman one day found both.

After that, I gave up and married a mostly silent man, and his mother made the case that silence masked strength. His mother loomed large in his secret mythology, I realized, because the only endearments forthcoming were baby talk—private noises he should keep to himself, I felt. If I pretended not to hear, his silence might be as exquisite as the emotion I ascribed to it. Then he disappeared for a few days. His feelings were so big he couldn't talk to me, his mother said. Or go to the store for items I needed. Or hold onto a job for long ever. I learned this and other unsettling facts silence had concealed. In time, I got divorced and ended up at a state university. My new house was deep in the country.

By then, I'd earned three degrees and published a few books. With nothing to distract me but the sound of birdsong and rushing wind, I worked. I also traveled to far-off conferences where every year or so I met a man. I substituted letters for physical contact longer than most women would because I lived so far from men I'd want to date. Verification of the spark—theory until words become flesh—required a road trip or plane ticket.

I got seduced in three genres: poetry, fiction, screenwriting. These men taught in provincial university towns too. We'd visit when we could. Mostly we gave good letter. No one takes a scrim of rapport, a rough draft of emotion, and turns it into love faster than a writer. *Poesis*: making something from nothing. I know the appeal of a sentence contorted to please its reader, a glimmer of sentiment solidifying to a point; I sent my Kama Sutra of syntax back. Love-letter lovers are like silent men who don't contradict the fantasy because love letters are edited. Loving an absent writer is like loving John Donne—though, in truth, no one was *that* good. Still, if bonding hormones are released by vivid memories artfully recounted, in time you remember the depiction, not the moment. As the number of letters surpassed hours spent together, the affairs fizzled.

At home, in the village near my house, I met men who might qualify as Byronic heroes in that their pursuit seemed unstoppable. One followed me to the hardware store, then to the grocery store, then to a gift shop that sold office supplies, then to the gas station, where I asked what he wanted. He stared at the ground and said he was hoping we could go for BBQ. Another time, I was at the post office, waiting in line to mail a package, and a man memorized my return address. How do I know? He told me the next day when he came to my house and recited a poem he wrote, its rhyme scheme dependent on words with "tion" endings, as in: *all this perspiration, due to love's vibration*. I wanted someone who wanted me so badly he'd say it. But I wanted to take him out in public.

The real value of epistolary love affairs became obvious once I had a daughter. By the time she was four, I'd gone on blind dates arranged by friends in neighboring cities. There weren't theaters or restaurants where I lived, and I didn't want dates coming to the house, serial "uncles" dragged though my child's life. A drive to a city was two hours round trip for me, twice that for a man who'd pick me up and drive me home. So the idea of dating was better than dating. Once, I had two hard-to-arrange dates with a novelist who lived in one of the cities. He told me he was going to Europe, but he wanted to stay in touch because he'd be back. I'd begun to develop early stages of a disease that made me too tired to do more than I already did: go to work, come home, grade papers, cook, get my daughter ready for bed, take her to school. But every night, I read e-mails from Prague. It was a conversation so good we had trouble ending it. Days before his return, he wrote to say he had a new girlfriend. Rereading all his letters, I pinpointed the weekend he'd met this new girlfriend. I didn't feel lovelorn. I felt like a story had ended abruptly.

I met my husband a few years later. He lived in one of the neighboring cities, and we both had school-age children, so we saw each other a few times a month. Sometimes we called each other. But phone conversation requires simultaneous free time. So we e-mailed.

What were his letters like? He spent his career writing statutes, so his letters demonstrated clarity, precision, and mastery of the subordinate clause, which he needed because he was always making provisions for unlikely exceptions to the rule. He'd write on the morning of a date to say: "We're ninety-five percent set, though there's a slim chance I might get called into the office, or my son or parents might need me." The first time he wrote this, I thought he was foreshadowing a late-in-the-day cancellation—because he'd lost interest or met someone new—but our dates came off without a hitch, except the day his mother needed to go to the ER. At first, this refusal to say *I'll be there*, and say instead *barring emergencies, I'll be there*, seemed like an occupational tic, not a sign of indelible loyalty ratified and henceforth applied. Then my illness got worse. I needed a six-hour test. He suggested my daughter go to the sitter's. He took the day off work.

A nurse shoved a tube into my arm. He looked unhappy. That night, he looked more unhappy. I worried what my test results might reveal. I also worried I'd let him see too much. With feigned nonchalance, I said, "You seem out of sorts." He took a long time answering, then said, "If it turns out you're really ill, I'd take care of you, my son, my parents, and I'd raise your daughter too. So, no, I don't feel romantic right now. I feel overwhelmed." I tensed up. I considered saying that I didn't need any of what he was offering, also that he had lousy bedside patter. Then I did say this, melodramatically, while cursing. I started a fight. Then stopped. I realized that all the well-chosen words, stowed in moldering envelopes, or on some now-discarded hard drive, never cared, not literally.

One summer, while I was traveling for work, he drove a hundred miles to my daughter's camp to deliver medicine she forgot to pack. He taught his son to drive, never once raising his voice. He held a gauze compress over his father's nosebleed one night from midnight until dawn. Sometimes I tell him how happy I am to be eating dinner with him, or reading books together by lamplight, or conferring about how to handle a tricky parenting moment. He'll say, "All that you said, yes. I'm happy too." My tribute—hopefully better than John Denver's, falling short of John Donne's—is imbalanced, so many paragraphs describing silent men who weren't strong, or articulate men who were or weren't but were too far away and, like me, not wary enough about the way that words aren't the adequate expression of every reality. A few paragraphs describe the love of my complicated days and nights, my husband, who promises only what he can and delivers more. He doesn't trust compliments, besides. So it's not for him I say that he's not silent, but he is strong. Saying so doesn't make *strong* stronger, yet I, word-junkie, just can't stop.

Trouble in Mind

I

Like many college girls in the late-1970s, the days of yore, I listened to Bonnie Raitt's covers of traditional blues songs about male sexual conquest with inverted gender references that meant she was singing about female sexual conquest. She also covered Sippie Wallace's unapologetic songs about female desire. This music implied that women could act and could avoid being acted upon. In 1977, if my acquaintance hadn't become my rapist, I might have initiated sex. *Technique ain't tough if you care enough*, Sippie Wallace. This proviso unique to acquaintance rape—that I might have wanted sex if I'd been consulted but was instead overpowered—is one reason the concept of consent stays muddled.

II

The June before my daughter's senior year of high school—she'd be leaving for college in a year, I realized—the velvety green days of summer were upon us, and I stood in my yard, looking at birds, bees, and blooms, and I was talking to one of the mothers I'd talked to for seventeen years, one of my daughter's friends' mothers. These were sometimes prickly conversations. If my daughter and her friend asked to go somewhere, the friend's mother and I would be briefly coparenting, but not coparent-

ing with love's encircling aura. We hadn't spent time agreeing and dis-
agreeing as we'd hammered out a set of shared bans and permissions, our
no way ever or *under these conditions* rules. We might not like or trust each
other, but here we were, determining rules for the weekend. Our daughters had asked to go camping alone in a spot neither pure woods nor an official campsite.

"Alone?" I said. "That seems unsafe. Maybe if more people come?
No. Still no. Because what if someone brings alcohol? There's potential
for trouble, like acquaintance rape." The mother nodded along until I
said "acquaintance rape." Then she gave me the same doubting, raised-
eyebrow look my best friend gave me in 1977. I should have exited the
conversation. In hindsight, I see I lacked foresight. In the moment, I was
annoyed that stranger rape was discussible but acquaintance rape still
wasn't. "Look," I said, "I teach at a university. One in four women is assaulted, most by someone they know, most before they turn twenty-five."
Our Title IX coordinator had addressed the faculty, asking those of us in
whom a victim might confide to report rape to her, adding that she'd in-
sure the victim's privacy even if the victim chose not to report her rape to
the police.

"Acquaintance rape is common," I said. "It's always been common."
Still no response. Though I habitually test my intuitions and knowledge
against vetted research, at that moment I decided, as I have too often in
life, to step out from behind data and history and speak up. I thought my
firsthand experience might swing the conversation. "Before they called
it that, acquaintance rape," I added, "no one called it anything." Still no
response. "I was raped," I said. I thought that if she knew acquaintance
rape could happen to someone she knew as mostly well-adjusted, also
gainfully employed, cautious in life if not in conversation, I'd make the
inconceivable real. I should have just said no, no to the camping, and
I did. But I thought it was better for the future, which belonged to our
daughters, if everyone would just acknowledge that acquaintance rape is
common.

III

I was acquaintance raped two years after the term "date rape" first appeared in Susan Brownmiller's *Against Our Will*, a book I never heard about at my small college, and eleven years before Robin Warshaw coined the term "acquaintance rape," in her book *I Never Called It Rape*. "Date rape" appeared first, but "acquaintance rape" covers all rape in a social setting, whether romantic interest between assailant and victim ever existed.

Had I been romantically interested? I can't say. A long *after* erodes a short-lived *before*.

In 1977, my best friend told me she'd have fought him off. "Until he'd have been screwing a corpse." Even at the time, I didn't think I'd have been better off dead. She said no one would have tried it on her because her boyfriend was well-known—everyone knew they were together!— and her way of carrying herself inspired respect too. I felt depressed and debased. I hadn't been unassailable. But her logic was. I hadn't inspired respect.

IV

I don't have contextual statistics from that long-ago Saturday night in northern Wisconsin, just memories. I wasn't drunk. More recently, as Robin Hattersley Gray wrote in the July 27, 2017, issue of *Campus Safety* magazine, "10 Sexual Assault Facts You Should Remember," 43 percent of campus rape victims are. I was raped by force, not incapacitation. Neither was my rapist drunk, though, according to Robin Hattersley Gray's data, 69 percent of campus rapists are. I'd worked the dinner shift at a restaurant. Then I went to a bar known for concerts by blues musicians stopping off between gigs in Chicago and Minneapolis. *I got that thang that make a bulldog break his chain.* I thought that thang was a power that could attract and repel. It could tell a bulldog to scram.

There was no concert that night, and the bar was nearly empty.

It had been an unusually warm April day, a glimmer of spring drawing people away from usual haunts. I'd gone out that morning to look at a river, melting, rushing chunks of ice. I drove back to town and changed into a dress with mauve roses I'd sewn myself. I wore it with tights and boots that later hobbled me. The dress turned out to be less armor-like than I later would have wished. It wasn't revealing, just fancy for work. When I arrived, a chef shouted, "You're spring personified." I'd ditched my coat for a shawl.

I'd regret the shawl later too.

When I got off work, I felt too elated and carefree to go home. I decided to go for a drink. I was acquainted with a customer who sat at the bar. My roommate was popular, and this guy and his twin brother had visited her at our apartment. We started to chat at the bar, and maybe I told him I'd gotten off work too late to catch up with my friends, explaining why I was solo. I felt a happy surge of reinvention. I'd just broken up with a possessive, flunking-out boyfriend, so I wandered, not lonely, but flushed and calm from having walked for hours beside a fast, cold river earlier that day. My rapist conversed well enough that when the bartender said he was closing early, no customers, and my rapist suggested we drink a beer at a big house he shared with male roommates, I said yes.

According to Carol Bohmer and Andrea Parrot, writing for the U.S. Department of Justice's Office of Justice Programs in *National Criminal Justice Reference Service*, men in all-male settings are likelier to commit acquaintance rape. According to researchers Patricia D. Rozee and Mary P. Koss, writing for *Psychology of Women Quarterly*, all-male settings foster adversarial sexual mores. As for my emphasis on what I wore, that I was alone, that in my heart I believed I could get my wang dang doodle off or not, my decision and no one else's, note that "the promiscuity defense" by which the accused could argue the victim has had sex in the past and is therefore predisposed to have sex again—in short, that all a victim has to lose is her virginity—wasn't made inadmissible until the Federal Rule of

Evidence 412, Relevance of Alleged Victim's Past Sexual Behavior or Alleged Sexual Predisposition, was codified in 1978. A year too late for me.

I had to first stop by my apartment to let my dog out, I said. I couldn't stay out late because my parents were dropping by in the morning, passing through on a trip to somewhere. My rapist told me I'd have trouble parking at his house, and I didn't know where it was, so he'd follow me to my place, then drive me to his house and home again later.

At my apartment, I split a bundle of pussy willows (*Salix discolor*, "catkins") I'd picked that morning. In the North, pussy willows matter for spring like redbud trees do in the South. Their blooms appear before any leaves on vegetation. If you're thinking I shouldn't have offered a man a bouquet with the word "pussy" in it, in the North some churches display pussy willows on Easter. And symbolism was outside my rapist's ken. When I gave them to him in his car, he acted so dumb, so puzzled. I told him they were a sign of spring in a climate of winter, and I thought: he's not my type. Polite, I didn't tell him.

Not one of his roommates was home. He cracked beers, then lunged as if he'd studied farm animals: stay on no matter how she tries to kick you off. I smiled and shoved, good-natured rejection. I may have said something empowered. *Baby, you got to know how.*

Later, my best friend asked if I'd screamed for help. The house was empty, so no.

I pushed back and pressed my fingernails into his skin. The next day my head was bruised. My shoulder was sprained. I could have let him pull my hair out, my best friend reasoned, since hair grows back. But he'd pulled it fast and hard, so I shifted in whatever direction he pulled. I was standing up when he pinned me against a wall, one elbow in my chest, one knee in my abdomen. I remember this part every time I sew because I still don't reinforce side seams because they aren't usually subject to stress: he yanked up my dress, which tore at the sides. He pulled down my tights and jammed them around the tops of my boots with one foot.

I did bite him, but this was after he was raping me, maybe under the illusion he wasn't because he paused, that same dumb and puzzled look, then continued.

If I'd later had to prove I hadn't wanted sex—not just rougher sex than I'd anticipated—I might have had trouble explaining I wasn't afraid afterward, just in a hurry to leave. Three miles up and down hills, over a bridge, balmy daylight gone. I had on a dress ripped hem-to-waist, a shawl, no winter coat. He wasn't afraid either. He slept, snoring.

This was way before cell phones. I used a rotary phone to dial friends' numbers I could remember, lots of no answer no answer. This was before answering machines or voicemail. I awoke one friend, and I'm certain I didn't say "rape," just "emergency," that I needed a ride, and she said she didn't know how she could help because she had work in the morning. I set the receiver down to open the door to get the house number, and when I came back she'd hung up. I looked up and down the street to see if any house looked as if its inhabitants might be kind to a disheveled woman knocking, asking for a ride.

I banked on that moment when, after I bit him, he'd looked quizzical—as if my resistance was that faux-kind in pornography in which a woman likes simulated force and I'd taken pretense too far. I woke him and asked to go home. He dressed and got his keys. As he drove, he made small talk. I was silent. He looked confused and asked if it was the torn dress I minded. In front of my apartment, he smiled and said, "Thanks. I had a great time."

I slept little, rose early, bathed, dressed. My parents arrived. This would be their only visit to me at college. My new life confused them. My dad looked ill at ease. My mom, worried: "Are you working too hard?" Maybe, I said. I couldn't explain. *I went to some guy's house and he forced himself on me.* It would have ruined her day, week, year, epoch.

When my roommate got up around noon, I said, "Your friend." Because I don't want a libel suit now, a *he says* and *I say* duel made weirder by forty years' passage of time, let's say his name is Jack. He has that twin. Their real last name is Hoehl or Hohl or Hole.

I said to my roommate, "Jack Hole raped me last night." I thought I'd have to defend my word choice. She said, "Where?" I said I'd run into him at a bar. What bar? "That isn't his usual bar," she said. "I wonder what he was doing over there. His roommates and brother were camping," she added. "Maybe he stayed home but got bored."

I said the bar had closed early, so we'd gone to his house for a beer. She said, "That was your mistake." I'd barely met him, she pointed out. He'd never expressed interest in me in front of people anyone knew. I countered that she'd brought him to our apartment and introduced him. She shook her head. "You're twisting everything. That doesn't mean he wants to date you." She went to cook breakfast, then came back. "You know what, though?" She named another of her friends, a sophomore with vulnerable eyes, and let's call her Valerie Johnson. "He did it to Valerie Johnson. They were driving to a party at someone's camp house, and he parked in the middle of nowhere in woods and snow. He jumped her and kept on. She definitely didn't want it and cried, telling him no."

V

A 2005 study by clinical psychologists David Lisak and Paul M. Miller "Repeat Rape and Multiple Offending among Undetected Rapists," published in *Victims and Violence*, found that 6 percent of college men commit acquaintance rape, and 63 percent of these 6 percent are serial rapists. A 2015 study by Kevin Swartout et al., titled "Trajectory Analysis of the Campus Serial Rapist Assumption," published in the *Journal of the American Medical Association*, reports that 10 percent of college men commit rape, and 25 percent of these are serial rapists. Numbers of rapists and repeat rapists vary as much as methodologies, including how researchers phrase their questions.

A rapist isn't quick to admit that he's raped, as mine did not to me, and his after-the-fact patter suggested he didn't even to himself. The conclusion of these studies, many victims and fewer rapists, accounts for the design of most campus programs designed to raise rape awareness: many victims and a few opportunistic rapists. A friend went to college years after I did. She said, "We had posters. The message was how women steer clear."

Rape prevention is still women's work. A sad and furious meme says it all: "Don't teach women not to get raped. Teach men not to rape." Yet, whether campus rapes are committed by a wider variety of men (75 percent of 10 percent of college men are one-time rapists, Swartout et al., 2015) or by fewer men (37 percent of 6 percent are one-time rapists, Lisak and Miller, 2005), serial acquaintance rape is frequent enough. Serial acquaintance rapists so lack what the rest of us call a conscience that they might be beyond education. We protect ourselves from them as we protect ourselves from any danger, hoping a little vigilance will prepare us. Still, we get ambushed.

Recent campus programs try to reach potential one-time acquaintance rapists who might otherwise see acquaintance rape as youthful hijinks, a drunken mistake, or a failure to communicate. It's probably too soon to know if any program prevents rape. According to a 2015 National Public Radio story, "Campus Rape Reports Are Up," between 2008 and 2012, campus rape in the United States increased 49 percent, data that suggests campus rape is growing more common or—good news—that more rapes are reported. Yet a 2014 study commissioned by the Association of American Universities, "Climate Survey on Sexual Assault and Sexual Misconduct," using a different methodology, found that most campus rapes, 72 to 95 percent, are not reported.

VI

When I confided in my best friend in 1977, her script came from old-fashioned movies: an innocent schoolmarm gets raped by a known outlaw. I told other friends, hoping for solidarity. One confided she'd been "fucked while passed out" and when she came to it wasn't the guy she'd gone out with, though she guessed he'd had at her first, and I thought my rape had been (this word, so inadequate) better. Another woke having sex she wouldn't have had if she'd been conscious, and we discussed whether to call this rape.

But most friends blamed my naiveté (I should have seen it coming), either that or my lack of naiveté. One said, "You know you like those records by those horny women singers."

Bonnie Raitt had led me to the harder stuff. Sippie Wallace, Koko Taylor, Big Mama Thornton, Laverne Baker, Big Maybelle, Ida Cox, Ruth Brown. They covered men's songs, angry or blue that a woman was mean, spent too much, didn't make love often or with enough skill. When women sang them, they became women's songs, angry or blue that a man was mean, spent too much, didn't make love often or with enough skill. Songs about a no-bullshit line a woman was drawing in the sand ("Walking Shoes," "Ain't Gonna Be Your Sugar Mama," "Don't Mess with the Messer"), songs about desire that better be met with finesse ("I Need A Little Sugar in My Bowl," "Hoochie Coochie Gal," "Too Many Men," "You Can Have My Husband but Please Don't Mess with My Man"), were a mirage: a gender-neutral economy in which women gave as good as they got.

A misinterpretation of a song lyric is an auditory Freudian slip.

Bonnie Raitt covered "Love You Like a Man" as "Love Me Like a Man," converting the singer from a man promising technique and respect into a woman who wants technique and respect. After I heard the verse about lovers who'd put themselves above her, their souls up on a shelf, and now she wants a man to rock her like her backbone was his own, I thought the simile in the title meant, not that the man should love her like he was a man, but like *she* was a man. Love Me Like a Man Expects to Be Loved.

VII

Campus was small. Jack and his twin were identical. They had matching late-model cars, the same haircut, the same distinctive laugh. Once, I changed directions so I wouldn't pass him or his brother holding court on steps in front of a classroom building I needed to enter. I slipped and fell. I kneeled, trying to stand, my backpack slipping, and glanced up. He glanced down, then away. Or not. To this day, I don't know if it was Jack or his brother, the other Hole. I've googled him. One social media profile has the right geographical details, yet the photo isn't of a human face but a navy blue mechanical pencil with a pink nub, an eraser, on top. Most people won't see this navy blue pencil as blue-veined, scorekeeping, revisionist, simplistically and aggressively phallic. I do. Symbolism, my forte. Yet that might not be his social media profile. There are many Jack Holes.

VIII

If my best friend's response in 1977 came from a mid-twentieth-century script featuring villains and virgins, my daughter's friend's mother's response forty years later came from psychotherapy. After a shuddering pause, she said, "That must have been hard." But my point isn't old hardship. I want my hindsight to become someone else's foresight. I want acquaintance rape to stop being the victim's fault, the victim's shame, for women to warn and help each other. Statistics suggest that if an acquaintance rapist succeeds once, he's likely to rape again, perhaps developing a better strategy for finding opportunities and victims. Law professor Jed Rubenfeld wrote a *New York Times* op-ed "Mishandling Rape" in which he correctly said that campus rape prevention has failed, too much talk about sex and alcohol, that prevention occurs only when victims trust jurisprudence.

But Department of Justice statistics, reported as " Campus Sexual Violence: Statistics" by the Rape, Abuse & Incest National Network, are dismal: 34 percent of all rapes—on and off campus, stranger and acquaintance rape—get reported; 6 percent lead to arrest; 1 percent to prosecution; less than 1 percent lead to conviction. Most rapes occur without witnesses, so if an arrest leads to trial, which isn't a given, a trial devolves into a credibility contest in which the scripted imitation of truth matters more than truth. And we discredit acquaintance rape victims for having known their assailants, though the thieved sometimes know their thieves and no one objects to that.

Trust in jurisprudence means trusting that a rapist will be arrested, prosecuted, convicted. As Department of Justice statistics clarify, the chances of that are slim, slimmer, slimmest. The world promised me autonomy, I felt. But even now if someone forcibly takes this from a woman, recourse succeeds not even 1 percent of the time. We have a name for this crime, but we don't yet have a legal strategy because definitions of consent are still tenuous, because laws used to prosecute acquaintance rape are amended versions of older laws never intended to cover acquaintance rape. Due process remains unlikely.

My daughter's friend's mother eyed me warily, worried I'd maybe cross the yard to warn our daughters—laughing and talking on the porch, hoping we'd say yes to camping—not to go alone (stranger rape) nor with acquaintances (acquaintance rape), and tell my cautionary tale. No. We can't scare our daughters with their lives starting, college next, lives for which they need hope and trust. But they also need suspicion and fear. They'll need to predict the future in order to walk into it or away from it as needed. So they won't be raped, or, if they are, won't be criticized for having failed to foresee the rape.

That day, I didn't tell my daughter and her friend I was raped because I'd be the worst messenger: stuck in my past, their prehistory, clueless about how nice people are! Most are. Most college men never rape: 90 percent (Swartout) or 94 percent (Lisak and Miller). Yet, according to Centers for Disease Control and Prevention's "Preventing Sexual Violence Fact Sheet," 29 percent of women are raped. My advice? It's new-fashioned. Men, stop. *Theory*. It's old-fashioned. Women, be as wise as you can be. *Practice*.

IX

I wasn't blue always. My campus rape didn't ruin my life. But at times I've found being a woman exhausting. Once, living in a duplex with cheap doors and locks, I woke to guys who lived down the street, standing on my sidewalk, shouting: "Girl in the brown house, come out and play." Maybe this was adorable, and I should have opened the door and made some new friends. I sat in the dark until they left, then tried to sleep. For years, I had a dream about my door to the outside being crashed open by wind, lightning, force. Studying for my PhD exams one year, hours every day, I started to study on my front steps after the weather turned sunny—until a man parked his car, came up the sidewalk, said he'd seen me alone every day, that we should be acquainted. I didn't study outside again. A few years later, I was a young, professional homeowner sitting on my own porch, in the dark, because I felt cozy in the dark, not spotlighted. A man materialized. He said his mother, my neighbor, knew me. We were acquainted. When I sat on the porch after that, I listened for the crackle in the dark, a broken twig, warnings that might alert me.

I went to a professional conference in an idyllic setting, white clapboard cabins in verdure, a conference known for its famous and hard-drinking attendees. (*Don't tell me about the life you've led. Don't try to drink me into bed.*) My cabin door had a flimsy hook-and-eye latch, and I listened one night as a man shouted I was a bitch holding out. This sounds uncourageous, but I spent the rest of the conference near a male colleague I trusted, signaling my status as "taken." When I got married, I noted the same side-effect: taken.

As victims go, at my age I'm statistically improbable now. But forty years later, I want every young woman to know, secondhand, what I know firsthand. On paper, women have power against their assailants.

In fact, they don't. Despite the studies, the data, the scholarly articles, the establishment of a Title IX task force that counts rape but doesn't suggest how to prevent it, acquaintance rape is common, and women don't often report it because they hear horror stories about indifference and harassment, deciding that a less than 1 percent shot at justice isn't worth the price. My sense of safety wasn't compromised that night but reconfigured to match reality. This isn't the conclusion I want, but I remained as afraid as the world still requires a woman to be.

My Life as an Aeolian Harp

In Kansas, in sweltering summers and only at night, I wore dancer's leotards with spaghetti straps or intricate strings lacing corset-like across my back. This was the early 1980s, when what people called "women's liberation" was somehow linked to "sexual liberation," not the same, not exactly, and many women wore strappy leotards as fashion then, the disco era, or skimpy tanks with short-shorts, the fitness craze. But August through May, I covered up. I was earning a master's degree in English with a newfangled emphasis in rhetoric I'd been told suited my career plan as I'd described it to a professor at the tiny state university I'd attended: to teach at a community college in a location so backwater no one else would want the job. I kept my aspirations lowkey because I lacked confidence, positive self-image, all that. And I was pragmatic. Men had a leg up in most professions.

Clothing and makeup choices for women who wanted careers were hotly debated. A woman should be attractive but not too. For all the chatter about women's sex appeal destabilizing the workplace, what I saw in this first phase of my long apprenticeship was that professors—all but one male, and she who wasn't taught children's lit and wore calico dresses with doily-like collars—were mostly helpful. Only a few signaled sexual interest.

Half my classes were in rhetoric. The rest were the old-school study of English. History & Theory of Grammar. Old English as a Foreign Language. And scads of enticing literature courses. Literature thrilled me, but I didn't see how to monetize it. Rhetoric didn't thrill me, but it's been long-term useful ever since with random tetchy neighbors or colleagues.

At first, I was a newlywed with no future plans to earn a PhD, inadvisable. You move for the degree, then for the job, hard on the husband. My husband left me, so a few years later I was free to attend a PhD program, where male students outnumbered female. But at this master's degree program in Kansas, most incoming students were women—unprecedented, our professors told us at a welcome-new-students party in someone's unlit backyard. Then they turned away and spoke to each other. Their wives, faculty wives, voices disembodied in the dark, made small talk. I'd moved there from Wisconsin, so when a mystifying screech split the air, I asked if wires on utility poles had shorted out. It's a cicada, a faculty wife said. Did I know the Greeks believed cicadas were humans the Muses had persuaded to sing who stopped eating and sleeping, and they died for loving singing and sang from the afterlife? I felt vaguely pleased, sacrificial death for art.

Fast-forward a year. I was separated not divorced, wearing strappy leotards for athletic dancing in clubs, night life. But summers in Kansas are incandescent heat radiating from earth and pavement, and one day I wore a merely sleeveless leotard with an airy skirt as I sat in an armchair upholstered in teal moiré. Other students looked dewy and fresh in shoulder-baring dresses and tank tops. This was in Dr. Newton's living room, where he was teaching a summer-session film studies class, Propaganda in Pornography, because the department didn't own a VCR. I heard Mrs. Newton upstairs, her sewing machine's whir.

Dr. Newton, an elf-like man in a guayabera shirt and khaki shorts, delivered introductory remarks before hitting "Play." His main subject was the English Romantics, and I wished we were studying that, not movies from a sketchy video rental store. But my most intellectual classmate had persuaded me we'd be opposing the objectification of women.

Darkling I listen.

I have been half in love with easeful Death.

I excelled at Romanticism, and I admired John Keats, whose imminent death, his constant companion by the year of his miracles in the form of odes, which was the year he was twenty-three, as I was then, became his muse. He had ravishing thoughts, rhymes, meter. Wordsworth? The landscape mirrored his soul, blah blah. "The Prelude" more like "The Delude," I felt. Shelly's ideas were innovative. His poetic technique, not so much. Coleridge's druggy hallucinations with their coded messages reminded me too much of my college boyfriend.

I'd had to write my final on "Kubla Khan." I sometimes still recite this poem in stentorian tones. The best argument for the study of literature is that you stock your brain with words and ideas you want or at least don't mind. *In Xanadu did Kubla Khan a pleasure dome decree*, I think, washing windows, long sweeps with a squeegee. This poem teeters between dread and bliss; surging and fading; holiness and tumult. In life, we teeter between pure states, risky, because pure-anything is obsession, as I wrote in my final. I segued to Coleridge's metaphor for creativity, a harp on a windowsill with its strings vibrating in breezes and gusts like the poet quivering with every disturbance. Overreaction to disturbance, "sensibility," was life-force amplified and a sign of superior intelligence.

I didn't add, having already strayed off-topic, that if you had "sensibility" in later eras, let's say in the 1980s when I was writing my exam, you were "high-strung," not a compliment, though I'd heard a man on a talk show say of course high-strung Jane Fonda exercised so much, and he kept his eye out for women like that because they're excitable in bed.

In Dr. Newton's living room, ballpoint pen in hand, legal pad in lap, I watched *Looking for Mr. Goodbar*, not good, not pornography, but this was the first day, and he was easing us in. He'd said to note how the plot punishes the female protagonist for casual sex. Here was the course rationale: to assert women's equal right to sex. I didn't like for my critical exegeses to be so immediately relevant. I wanted to be swept away from my problems as I worried about characters or authors, trusting that wisdom I gleaned would stay with me until I needed it later, not for a current and overwhelming quandary. I wondered if anyone else in Dr. Newton's living room had spent time like the movie protagonist: wanting sex with love, but love worth having is scarce, so she had just sex.

Sex in the movie looked like athletic dancing, writhing, panting, unbroken eye contact. Before my brief marriage, I'd sometimes had sex like that. Once in a while, it was great. If it was, the two of you ran circles around each other, showing up at the same place, acting aloof, approaching, retreating. Some men looked confused. Did they want love? They had no idea. Some did, and maybe I didn't. Some worried I'd try to oversee their clothes, their meals, their lives. Scheduling seemed to require an appointment secretary. I'd tell someone I wasn't available one night but would be later, and he'd get mad. I wondered: Was all the fuss finding sex why I'd gone and married a man I barely knew?

Looking for Mr. Goodbar doesn't just depict the sexual revolution, Percy Bysshe Shelley's revived for the 1960s and just beyond: post-pill, pre-AIDS. It points out that even if a woman won't get a bad reputation, pregnant, or lastingly syphilitic, she can get killed.

During class discussion, I said moodily the protagonist wasn't bad, just unlucky because no one in the movie was worth loving, including the husband-material guy, also unlucky to have encountered a psychopath, statistically improbable—like *Anna Karenina* or *The Awakening*, I added, this levying the death penalty for sex, sacrificial death for pleasure. My argument wasn't bolstered by the fact that the movie was based on a true story. "She asked for her bad luck," said a student with curly short hair and a denim dress. Her mother, auditing, came to class with her. The mother nodded vigorously. No one wanted to contradict a mother, so discussion stalled. Dr. Newton was one of those professors who, like dog owners endorsing the "let them fight it out" theory of dog obedience, never intervened.

The next movie in Dr. Newton's living room was *Barbarella*.

As it happened, I and millions of women my age owned *Jane Fonda's Workout*, a vinyl LP. I'd first learned this workout from a neighbor who'd learned it at the university rec center, then bought the LP, taped it, invited women to the VFW hall and taught us, using her husband's tape player. Working out was meant to improve how we looked in scanty clothes, but the sequence of exercises eased my muscles, taut due to studying and taut due to wide-ranging angst. Jane Fonda's first husband, Roger Vadim, directed her in *Barbarella*: "She cannot relax." Her second husband, Tom Hayden: "High-strung as any wire."

Barbarella is a male fantasy, high-tech orgasms perpetrated on a woman, and when she gets kidnapped then rescued, her rescuer, a man, gives her old-fashioned ones. Yet, as Dr. Newton said, this featuring of female pleasure was an emerging hopeful sign, progress.

The next movies weren't mainstream. The mother of the curly-haired student stopped coming. We saw some my brain has blocked. I recall scenes from *Behind the Green Door*, which Dr. Newton described as "a woman-centric quest movie" because female characters seek pleasure. What they find, or perform, is anatomically inaccurate: inexplicable orgasms caused by men rubbing against women's bodies in zones not known to be erogenous. My most intellectual classmate said this movie merely repeated tropes from male pornography, which was clearly the only pornography. "If offered the opportunity, would women even want to objectify men?" she asked, pen poised in air. The curly-haired student said it was all violent. At first, I thought she maybe meant male-female relations were inherently violent, like Andrea Dworkin five years later writing that "a normal fuck by a normal man" is invasion. Maybe the curly-haired student was leading us to radical insight? Then she said only married sex can be good.

The last movie of the summer was the exploitation movie *Snuff*, directed by a man who'd heard of Third World films in which actresses don't act out their death by murder during sex, though they're told they will. They're killed while the camera rolls. *Snuff*'s marketing: "The film that could only be made in South America where life is CHEAP." Dr. Newton assured us this was false advertising meant to induce more people, aroused, outraged, or curious, to rent the movie. It was just pretend: murder as cinematic climax; stillness-of-death as falling action; an actress posed as a blood-spattered Lady of Shalott. I sat in the teal moiré armchair with my legal pad. With my suspension of disbelief, the poetic faith Coleridge said is required for what German Romantics called *einfühlung*, or "feeling into" art, so that you believe the invented is real, Dr. Newton's distinction barely mattered.

Before I left Kansas, I tracked down the man I'd married and got him to sign divorce papers. I kissed two of my classmates. I slept with someone local I didn't like, nor he me, but we liked sex with each other, and I called him my boyfriend until I moved to a PhD program, to the confusing attention there from a handful of classmates and at least one professor. I met a man off-campus and coupled with him, until after I graduated and moved for a job, after which I dated someone almost but not quite old enough to be from another generation, who'd hear me use words he liked and try to use them: "persona" when he meant "personality," as in my "persona" seemed tense, he told me; or "hyperanalytic," as in my "persona" was "hyperanalytic." He'd suggest I'd feel better after I had an orgasm, and it turns out he was as good at facilitating these as Barbarella's rescuer.

Was this parity? If offered the opportunity, would women want to objectify men? I didn't want to be played. I wanted to be the object of the attentions I wanted while being as little objectified as possible, a dilemma at the heart of what we now call agency: choosing an option from a narrow and preset range. *Plus ça change, plus c'est la même chose.* The immutability of history and habits. I got my needs met in a world at odds with my own best interests, a man's world. Of course, I had to live "socially and gregariously," as Nietzsche wrote about why we agree to communal versions of truth we know don't describe our experience. Nothing in pornography class taught me about agency, its catch-22.

Later, I was living in Texas, with its sweltering summers, and one day, I was in a grocery store parking lot, wearing an airy skirt and strappy top. A man stepped out from between parked cars to say, "I like how you carry yourself," and lifted a big bag of dog food out of my shopping cart into my car trunk while asking me out, adding that he didn't like dating women with careers, so uptight, and I probably had one, but he hoped I at least didn't have kids, because career women with kids were especially uptight, so count him out. I thought how often I'd been called high-strung or its equivalent, how most women are. "Wound up tighter than a ten-day clock," a male colleague likes to say about another of our colleagues, a woman. About him, people say: good leader, eye on every detail.

Jane Fonda in *Barbarella*—her costume a fancy leotard—is an imperiled heroine, not a superhero. I started doing her workout before I saw *Barbarella* and somehow didn't stop. Friends tell me to try CrossFit, hot yoga, belly dancing, weight lifting, whatever's new, but I don't. Jane Fonda, old enough to be from another generation, is "male-oriented" as we used to say about women who arrange their lives for men. When I listen to interviews with her, I hear how imperfectly she's internalized the recurring censure for taking action, the recurring praise for refraining from taking action. No wonder she exercises. For years, her workout has reliably released my muscles, taut due to my wide-ranging angst and taut due to my merely repetitive stress from typing too much.

When turntables became obsolete, I taped the workout onto a cassette. When cassette decks became obsolete but before I burned a CD, I exercised by borrowing my daughter's Playskool tape player. In the streaming years, my new husband uploaded the album onto iTunes. I know it by heart, so I don't hear Jane's instructions or the passé disco beats as I exert and flex. During the longest sets, I sometimes assess my epochs. Ab crunches twenty through twenty-nine, I think how I felt in my twenties: all grad school and job interviews, no confidence. Ab crunches thirty through thirty-nine: learning to be boss of my life, boss of my life. Ab crunches starting at forty, I think: learning to be a mother, mother, mother. As the count nears fifty, I think: more needs met more often, more.

I've decided this about *einfühlung*. In art, we feel some of what we dread. A narrative without dread falls flat. But too much is too much. My husband recently refused to keep watching a reputedly great movie because the adult actors convincingly played teenage characters having sex, and my husband, suspending disbelief, felt wrong watching teenagers have sex. I won't watch movies with heroines objectified-unto-death. No sexy true loves dying in hospital beds. No eroticized corpses in police procedurals, pornography for Puritans—viewers get titillated and then self-absolve when the murderer is caught.

I trust that Dr. Newton, well-schooled in his "auxiliary research interest," as academics say, had good intentions. But every woman in the room already knew more than he did: that free love is freer for men. We walked carefully to cars in dark parking lots. If we left a dance club at night with a man, we knew we'd already consented. Men could hurt us. Some of them would. Dr. Newton might have described *Snuff*, not assigned it.

That afternoon, I doodled on my legal pad, staring at it or around the room. The curly-haired student was tearing rippled strips of paper out of her spiral-bound notebook. Another woman with a plastered-on smile smiled at the wall. Given what we'd keep learning about what some men really want, it's a wonder any of us ever sorted out how to have sex that gave us pleasure, but most of us probably did. The TV connected to the VCR emitted an aria of screams, and my pen slipped off my legal pad and onto the teal moiré armchair. I heard Mrs. Newton's sewing machine upstairs, its whirring and clicking, and wondered if I should stop after class to tell Dr. Newton I got black ink on his armchair. He seemed to be having second thoughts, too, his expression startled and blank.

A Formal Feeling

Aunt Alvina's sons and daughters and the spouses of her sons and daughters were assigned the choir loft for solidarity as they wept while remembering and roiling with feeling and trying not to, or not too much, to avoid entering the void without end while on display, next of kin. I arrived with my stepson and daughter. My husband brought his father, Aunt Alvina's brother, having first gone to the assisted living to shave and dress him. Then he'd wheeled him to the pickup, lifted him in, collapsed the wheelchair, and he drove seventy miles to the church where he put his father back in the wheelchair and brought him inside to see, first, a table with mementos, including an old news story about the Agricultural Association award Aunt Alvina once won for her hens. In the photo, she smiles while driving a tractor, the story a record of her unforced joy at the cycle of sowing, growing, reaping, and dormant stillness of winter when, on a farm, you just wait: renewal.

Next my husband wheeled his father to the coffin to be near the body. Some death rituals emphasize proximity to the body. So peaceful, people say. Inert, I say. In the old days, there was no avoiding the body. People died at home. People who knew them washed and dressed the bodies. A body helps you know it's no longer the person you loved or feared or blinked back anger at. The body is the site of memories already fading, and soon you remember only having remembered, and the person slips away, a changing idea.

Grieving means *carrying a burden*, and the idea that grief will go away and stay away is new. *Closure* once meant *wall*. Then it became a word to describe the end of conflict or the end of a poem or symphony. According to Google Books Ngram viewer, an online tool that graphs the rate of a phrase's appearance over time, *closure to grief* first appeared in print in 1982, then became commonplace. In 1982, I was a few years older than the students I taught in freshman English, and our textbook had themed units of short readings to inspire paper topic ideas, and one unit called Death & Dying included Tolstoy's "The Death of Ivan Ilyich," which students hated, too nebulous, and an excerpt from Elisabeth Kübler-Ross's book about stages of grief (denial, anger, bargaining, depression, acceptance), which they loved as if I'd given them a study guide to help them ace the final.

Back then, I was a death-virgin, but I scoffed, all the same. Don't expect a grief manual, I might have said. Grief is surely mysterious, each experience unique, closure an aspiration only. Maybe I shivered, aesthetic chills. Death as class discussion was exciting. Séances at slumber parties used to be. It's all tingling theory when you're young, death an altered state. My stipulations turn out to be true. I aim for closure anyway, to begin to understand precise ways that feeling *bereft*, which means *having been robbed*, will go on forever.

I live in a city but I've so far had all my death experiences in small towns, where funeral directors often know the dead person and loved ones, lives lived before and after, who on the list of survivors fared better or worse. A small-town funeral director sees that grief isn't one grief but a confluence, old griefs sluicing into new griefs, many griefs merged.

My mother died in a small town. She was widowed three years and newly remarried. Her second husband of twenty years had died, and she'd moved to marry this third husband, also widowed. They'd been in love and hurried to marry because "death do you part" was a deadline. Her out-of-the-blue dying months later came too soon for me, too soon for my sister in a different way, and too soon for the husband, who seemed inflamed, in mutiny at this new levy, another death, another reason to hate his first wife's dying.

My mother's husband made a bleak joke to the funeral director: "What about a discount for repeat customers?" Then left the room and cried robustly. Next, he came back and worried aloud that since my sister and I didn't know his family members, arriving with cakes and casseroles, we'd feel worse. But my mother's funeral had to be somewhere.

This family was so good at gathering. When my own family gathered, no matter each individual's serene intention, a fracas befell. For instance, at my brother's wedding, my dad fell down due to drinking, car keys flying into the snow. I saw them land and grabbed them. Car keys in snow are no joke at night, limited visibility. My stepmother, who was still my dad's girlfriend then, had been upset for hours because—in deference to my mother, who'd hoped my dad's girlfriend wouldn't attend the wedding, but my dad insisted—someone asked my stepmother to step aside during a family photo. I realize she felt excluded. She thought I wanted the keys to be high-handed. She slapped me and took them.

These run-ins aren't one person's fault. We start with small talk about happy or funny shared memories because that's what we have in common. This restarts old ways of interacting, and surprise, the bad chemistry, the explosion. I bow out of most family gatherings.

For my own Kodak moments, like my daughter's naming ceremony or my wedding to a good man when I was middle-aged, I have small celebrations and send announcements later. I've sometimes invited my sister, but word gets out and they all arrive, jolly until miffed. So I was relieved my mother died in a far-off place among people who weren't sad for her because they didn't know her but sad because they loved her husband, who was sad. My sister and I were sad. So were well-mannered aunts and uncles, my mother's best siblings, arriving in rental cars from the airport a hundred miles away.

My mother's husband told the funeral director to defer to my sister and me, our desires. So, at a rite I'd never heard of, a prayer vigil at which the coffin stays closed, not to be opened until the funeral two days later, a rite apparently always on the slate when someone in my mother's new family died, the funeral director took my sister and me aside to say that, due to the prednisone with which doctors tried to save our mother's life, her body was deteriorating quickly. He'd tried every mortuary science technique. He suggested a closed-coffin funeral and those who wanted should see the body soon, in private.

After the vigil, we sipped coffee and ate cookies. No one wanted to see the body except my uncle. Everyone else said: "I'll recall her as she was." The funeral director, a source of expertise, stood near me. I murmured that I'd had a boyfriend who died and I never went to his funeral. I stopped before adding that our relationship ended before he died, none of that hyped closure, just shrieking and insisting on my part and what we now call stalking on his part. His mother found me and called, hysterical. For years I dreamed about him, twenty-something, tuning an electric guitar, clicking through lines of coke, voicing his grudging approval as I became a graduate student, an author, a professor, a mother.

The funeral director said if I had a glimmer of an urge to see my mother I should.

People often have regrets about deaths in the past, he added.

In the material realm, these recurring dreams about the dead must be long-term memories stored in your brain mixing with recent memories from a different emotional index, old memories binding with new, and you're forced to reconsider the old in light of the new and vice versa. Like I wished my dead mother knew my baby daughter longer, and I found my mother in a room in my house that's also a room in her new husband's house and also a room in the house where she grew up, my grandparents' house, so three rooms fused. My mother, holding my daughter, is not alive. But she has a body. Not for long, she says. It's spongy. She says to touch her arm, see? The brain has no choice but to blend new information and old information and tell a story, making the dead into minor characters. But if you believe in the unverifiable, dreams are a communiqué from far-off exile.

At the viewing of my mother's body in a small room, I felt nothing. She'd been changed by the prednisone. She was no one I'd met. She was too big. And beauticians who arrive at odd hours, working from photos, get it wrong. But the fingertips were hers. Fingernails press down and contain the swelling. As a child, in church or at a concert, during sermons or music, I'd loved my mother's hands, translucently thin skin due to housework, smooth due to her almond-scented hand cream. I'd trace the veins, the knuckles, the oval nailbeds. After a few minutes, my uncle sighed. "Yes, that's her," he said.

My husband steered my father-in-law's wheelchair back to our pew at Aunt Alvina's funeral, only two weeks after his own mother's funeral. During Aunt Alvina's, my father-in-law would have preferred to obey the unwritten ban against public displays of grief. But he couldn't stop himself from crying harder than Aunt Alvina's sons and daughters, nearer next of kin. At his wife's funeral, only two weeks earlier, he'd braced himself, stoic. Now he was like my mother's husband: a death for which he'd prepared and then another, no warning, the second time like rain falling on rivers already swollen, cresting.

Aunt Alvina, age eighty-seven, had lived alone, playing cards every Wednesday with her friends who hadn't yet died. "Oh the fun," she'd said once. "We laugh and laugh." Then she fell, and EMS took her to the hospital. Pain management usually works, though it muddies last words. It failed Aunt Alvina, who begged to die to end the pain, her daughter said. Hours of pain. A day, two days. She died. My mother-in-law's dying took longer.

My husband had sat with his father at his mother's deathbed on and off for weeks as she sometimes spoke before slipping back into a state like sleep. When she died, my husband began to plan the viewing, the funeral, gravesite prayers at the cemetery miles from town, and a reception at a nearby hall. He asked for my help choosing food, flowers, clothes.

At my mother-in-law's viewing, a tiny fracas befell. I'd told the small-town funeral director I didn't know what to do with the two corsages that came with the florist's package I'd ordered, and he explained that female next of kin and female dead wear them. As people arrived to show the dead person was known and loved, a woman who'd once been hired to help cook for my husband's parents when they got too frail brought another corsage she'd hoped to pin on my mother-in-law in her coffin. This woman was "not well," as the funeral director later put it. When she saw I'd already pinned a corsage on my mother-in-law's pink lapel, she shoved me. I felt startled in my black dress, shoes I'd polished, nylons I got at a grocery store, hoping to look right, to blend. She shouted I wasn't a real daughter-in-law because I hadn't been married long enough. This all felt vaguely usual to me except that kind people closed ranks, restoring calm.

Next, the funeral. Before it started, we were put in the choir loft: my husband, me, our children; my father-in-law; Aunt Alvina; and my mother-in-law's twin sister, Aunt Gladys, a recluse. The choir loft was for our distinction, immediate family. During the funeral, because our group was small, we sat in the front pew. Next, the gravesite. A hot wind blew across fields, whipping the canopy, sunshade the funeral director erected over folding chairs. This final rite—prayers and symbolic fistfuls of soil—was attended only by us and really old people, silent and still, as the roaring wind seemed to lift and rend the canopy.

Then we went to a hall to eat ham sandwiches and apple crumble. Friends and relations asked: How old was my daughter? My stepson? What subjects did each one like in school? They approved my answers, good answers, good children gleaming nearby, my daughter in a dress I'd just bought, my stepson in a new shirt, clothes they'd wear a few weeks later to Aunt Alvina's funeral but we didn't know yet. This was their first funeral, and they'd slipped out of their real ages, preteen and teen, to be solemn and helpful.

The crowd thinned, and my father-in-law said he didn't know what to think about now, if not his wife. Aunt Alvina, in the dress she'd wear in her coffin a few weeks later, but we didn't know, told him to assent to grief. She understood this season, its weather. One of my husband's uncles had quit attending funerals altogether, too many now, he'd said.

Weeks later at Aunt Alvina's funeral, my father-in-law said, "I don't understand." The new death, he meant, its timing. Tributary grief. He cried so hard that Aunt Alvina's daughter-in-law in the choir loft noticed and cried with him. People cry by contagion due to visuospatial neurons, mirror neurons that reflect social cues: they were born with hair-trigger neurons or grew up in chaos and developed them to detect signs of others' mood swings.

Emotional contagion is a crude form of empathy. The sight of someone crying accesses the second crier's warehouse of memories. I started crying with my father-in-law and Aunt Alvina's daughter-in-law. Sitting next to me, my daughter watched, confused, because I'd quashed impulses to cry at my mother-in-law's funeral, though I knew her better. My daughter had also seen my father-in-law cry less at his wife's funeral than he cried now. I cried with him, in concert. My husband avoided looking at us because he hopes never to cry. If I correctly interpreted glances from Aunt Alvina's sons and daughters in the choir loft, they saw my crying as proof I'd been a daughter-in-law long enough. They thought I cared about my father-in-law. I did. And I cast about for something dully mundane to think about so I'd stop crying at the funeral of a nice aunt by marriage.

Reasons for not crying in public are tacit, uncodified. Raw emotion disturbs the group, true. Seeing someone cry or yell at work or a party gives us pause. But someone yelling in public—lashing out—seems better tolerated than crying. Because yelling is maybe seen as out-of-control but not weak? Crying is abject. Since public crying is rare, there's no etiquette for responding. Tolerant body language? A no-information remark affirming the social contract? People who witness crying also worry it's a jealous bid for attention. The Greek city-state forbade crying. A man couldn't soldier while also weeping. Crying women were bad PR. Stoicism means defeating emotion for the greater good.

Some cultures encourage public grief, allowing that, even before biochemistry proved this, crying can help, releasing stress hormones, also allowing for the fact that crying en masse, like celebrating en masse, is the occasional expression of an emotion, that, once expressed, won't derail the collective. Discouragement of public grief seems rooted in fear of contagion, the barely articulated idea that if one of us cries then all of us might, crying too hard and too long, unable to work, raise our children, cook, clean, repair, endure.

During the days before my mother's funeral, many of us didn't know much about each other besides our professions. One of my mother's new husband's daughters, watching my sister and I arrange our mother's funeral (she'd not long ago helped arrange her own mother's), suggested that I, a writer, should write and deliver the eulogy. My sister agreed. I wrote a carefully partial account of my mother's life: warm generalizations followed by warm examples, nothing woeful or grim to alarm the family into which she'd married.

I was out-of-body, watching myself read while staring at people's foreheads to create the illusion of eye contact. I fended off vagrant memories. The tender look on her face when I'd read a poem I'd written for a grade-school pageant. Or when she'd yelled when I was seventeen and on the verge of serious trouble. Or when she'd waved a sad and terrified goodbye from the end of her tether, her driveway. As the funeral ended, I was in front with the priest, recalling my mother once saying that family members shouldn't be pallbearers, undue pressure, a rule from her childhood. I saw my brother across the church. He'd arrived the night before. A tear rolled off his nose as he reeled, hoisting the coffin.

But at the prayer vigil two nights before her funeral, I had no assigned role, no assigned seat. Packed in the middle—my new stepfather was well-liked and his extended family huge—I had the illusion I'd disappeared, anonymous. The best argument against public crying is that even if you bring tissues—if you have, is the crying premeditated?—they turn into messy pulp. Crying activates nasolacrimal glands. People near you cringe. Only my mother's husband's youngest daughter, who'd been a teenager and still at home when her mother died (so thinking about her mother and not mine), cried too. Later, my uncle asked unironically if I was sick. My aunt, in an immobility of austere remembering, hurried away. She believed, as my mother had, that public crying is a hygienic and moral hazard.

My mother's second husband's funeral was also planned quickly. He had a heart attack in the car while she was driving, and she asked someone to call me to get on a plane to help with his funeral. My mother had married him twenty years earlier, and I hadn't seen her in person in a long time, but we talked by phone. At work, I requested days off, and I asked a neighbor to feed my pets. Both my supervisor and neighbor asked me who died. Stepfather, I said. They paused—no auto-rejoinder—and expressed basic sympathy.

A few years after he died, when my mother died, conventional sympathy was consolingly true if cryptic, aspirational. Aspiration gets you through when you're in shock. But conventional expressions of sympathy jarred when my stepfather died. "May good memories comfort you soon," my neighbor said. "No good memories at all," I answered. She looked startled. I'd sounded hostile, so I added, "I won't need any comfort."

My neighbor said smoothly, "You were estranged."

When my mother married this husband, I was a young adult, still moving around. The two of them moved, too, to a small town in Arizona filled with people from the North who were sick of snow. He wanted no oversight—I mean my brother and sister who'd lived near and tried to get her out. From then on until he died, my brother and sister saw my mother on odd afternoons carved out when she and her husband traveled north to visit his children. Twice I traveled by plane to see her, sleeping in their guest room. Both times, I cut the visits short due to safety concerns. Failing to secure hers, I fled. I saved myself.

I saw her at a family reunion once. He'd dropped her off, staying in the car as she lifted her overnight bag out of the trunk. He felt her siblings looked down on him. They did. At my grandfather's funeral, my aunt said, he'd been mad my mother was focused on her father's death and not on him. He'd yelled during the gravesite praying and stalked away. At the family reunion, my mother and I greeted each other. In an instant of looking at each other's faces, I could see she regretted our lapsed in-person contact but felt this lapse was our private calamity, our secret to keep. My sister knew about the aborted visits because I'd called her afterward, crying. My sister sometimes called me, crying. Even my sister didn't quite know how little I'd seen my mother: the aborted visits; the one family reunion; and once my mother and this husband passed through a city where I lived, tense stopover.

My sister had been summoned to my mother's second husband's funeral too. We three sat in the front pew on one side and the husband's four children on the other. The funeral director had asked how many next of kin, and I'd paused, uncertain. He quickly suggested two front pews: equally honorary but separate. My mother knew some of her husband's children but not an out-of-contact daughter. One of the children led this daughter to the coffin. She looked at her father's body, screamed, collapsed on the floor. She implied ill of the dead. She made a fracas in front of the other attendees, most of them neighbors, who seemed surprised to learn my mother had children. "Daughters!" one said, gapemouthed. As the stepdaughter sobbed on the floor, my mother didn't cry. All week, she didn't cry. She shivered and talked fast, flitting from one odd subject to another.

But the stepdaughter's unhappiness set off a surge in me. I can't remember how hard I tried not to cry. My mother poked me, stern yet droll: "Do you need to visit the Ladies?" Wanting to please her, I visited the Ladies. Then I came back and cried anew. Her life, a big part of it, had been wasted by him. My life, a big part of it overlapping hers, had been wasted by him. She wasn't so delusional to think I was crying for him. Maybe she decided I was crying out of terror about the finality of death. She held my hand.

At his funeral, I cried for the lost years of my mother's life when she did without, the lost years of mine when I did without, bereft before she died. During her funerary week three years later, a genial if impersonal week with blanks to fill—typical behaviors and remarks for a typically grief-struck daughter—I thought how we'd have fared better if she'd had more time with this third husband I didn't know, but he seemed good, his family members I didn't know, but they seemed good. So I thought at another small church, in another small town, at a prayer vigil two nights before her funeral, at a ritual no one in our family knew. I cried, hoping she wouldn't mind. How implausible that she neither could nor couldn't? I cried in front of people who recoiled at my crying, crying while pried open. I cried for an hour. Then I fell in and never cried about her in public again.

But grief valves, spillways, opened a few weeks later. I lived in a small town, and my neighbor died. Like my mother's third husband's first wife who preceded my mother in death by a few years (dying slowly whereas my mother died quickly), like my mother-in-law who preceded Aunt Alvina in death by a few weeks (dying slowly whereas Aunt Alvina died quickly), my neighbor Clara Mae had been sick for a year, and my mother was healthy one day and dead the next. A first death for which you fortify, then another, the ambush. Except the order was reversed: my by-ambush death first, my readied-for death next. I'd brought Clara Mae meatloaf and roasts and soup for a year. She wasn't better, but she wasn't worse until the phone rang. Then she was dead just after my mother was.

I sat in back at her funeral. I brought my briefcase instead of a purse because it was big enough for a slim box of tissues and potentially copious discards. I'd stop-and-start-cried since the phone call. Years later, I told my husband about crying hard at Clara Mae's funeral, weeks after my mother's, and how, at its end, I'd hurried past her next of kin. I'd waved, embarrassed, disheveled, wet, and heard a stranger say: "Is that a daughter?" My husband understood why I'd hurried. He described the funeral of a friend, a man with three girlfriends, none of whom meant to vie for status as most affected, but their piled-upon bewailing and sniffling increased the immediate family's sadness and strain.

My husband and I were sitting at the kitchen table. Our light staved off nightfall. We ate hot soup, hot bread, winter fare. My husband recalled a funeral when he was ten, his grandmother on his mother's side, and back in the day when women's lives might fall out this way, she'd been a young mother when her husband sent her away to a mental institution after years of beating her into submission, maimed despair. My husband's mother and her twin sister, Gladys, born in 1926, swaddled together in a wicker basket, grew up without her. Her body came home to be buried, and every woman in the church sobbed while men looked away. "She'd been gone long already," I said. My husband nodded.

Crying in private never lasts long. I think of tasks to complete while also crying, maybe cleaning baseboards, reorganizing a cabinet, grading papers, and the crying stops. But the impulse remains, small, tight, a whirling pocket covered by daily stillness and rushing. At Clara Mae's funeral, a cascade overtook me. I wished to cry with strangers, though this would be onerous for the people who dislike crying, not due to repression, but rare people don't get a biochemical release and feel worse, not better, for having cried. We'd segregate, I decided, crying in distinct chambers, one for criers, one for stalwarts. I pictured a room in which we who wanted would unstop, convocation of sorrow, swarm of woe, pandemonium of laments, zeal for effusion, the dams opening, a mass grief-letting, letting.

––––––––

After Aunt Alvina's funeral, I felt lightheaded from having cried. My father-in-law felt weak. My husband says we went to the reception after Aunt Alvina's funeral, but I don't remember. We'd have seen the same people we'd seen two weeks earlier at the reception after my mother-in-law's, which I do remember. When I arrived at my mother-in-law's funeral reception, I saw my husband, suitcoat cast aside, broad shoulders in a white shirt, smiling at people who waved as he carried his father to the wheelchair. My husband had a fever. We'd risen at dawn to get ready, to get the family ready, and he told me he'd caught a bug at the hospital, the long hours, his mother's dying. A reception is refreshments and light conversation. The beloved is gone forever, yet people laugh and eat.

Because the hardest rites are over: the body at its viewing, familiar but strange; the body at church with emotive singing; the body lowering into the ground. I didn't see my mother's body into its grave. When the funeral was over, it had a train to catch. Her body was buried as per instructions from an old will, in a grave no one visits, in a town no one I know lives, in a plot bought by her cruel second husband. I sent her body off during a week of observances among strangers, observances that upheld me as I upheld them: structure against which I braced, my lack wider and deeper each new time someone dies.

After my mother-in-law and Aunt Alvina died, Aunt Gladys died. We'd talked by phone on Sundays. She told me about shopping for food and cooking, and I told her news about the children. She left home a final time, carried on a stretcher, asking the EMS man to go back for her curlers and makeup. The uncle who'd objected to the proliferating monotony of funerals died. My father-in-law—barely anyone left to attend his funeral—died.

I haven't deleted Aunt Gladys's number from my contacts, and when I see it, I think of her waiting for her squat, black phone to jangle alive. Last week, I dreamed I was at a professional conference where, in waking life, I see people I've known for decades, but I've lost track, and now and then, a formerly well-known face emerges into focus in a blur of unknown faces on an escalator rolling the other way or in a crowd pushing the opposite direction. I see my mother in the crush. We need to talk because I have much to tell her, I think. *Much*, I mouth as she passes. Because she can't hear. She smiles and waves and slips away.

I was still middle-aged when we arrived at my mother-in-law's gravesite during a drought, a heat wave, cornfields withering too soon. Old people in their best clothes sat in folding chairs under the canopy that whipped in hot wind. They wobbled to stand up and offer us their seats. My husband urged them to stay, but he wheeled my father-in-law under the canopy beside them. I held my husband's fever-hot hand, and the children, death-novices, pressed near. I didn't care about the propriety of crying or not-crying, but I stayed calm for them. Prayers began, and I watched the old people, their sere faces creased deep, each one of them remembering more griefs than I did yet, gleaming eyes impenetrable and mysterious over hidden, rapid, pooling, jammed-up, and unloosening grief.

The Wrong Conversations
about Hate Activity

In the spring of 2017, an editor asked me to write an essay about porches with an upbeat takeaway, and I thought porches let us navigate the zone between public and private life and connect, but I'd just sat on my porch and conversations had sent me back inside, feeling scalded. Small talk had taken a dark turn, my fault. Most people can't hear you have a problem without suggesting a quick fix because they want to make you feel better. I tried to write about porches and ended up writing about social life. I tried to write about social life and ended up writing about social media, where we also navigate the zone between what's public or private and connect or don't. On social media, our virtual porch, we converse with friends, friends of friends, that somebody no one knows, and decide who to wave over and who to dodge. People in whom I tried to confide looked like they might be company.

The first incident I tried to describe occurred on November 11, 2016, the Friday night after the presidential election. My daughter, a college freshman, lived a few hours away. While she was asleep, her car was jumped on or slammed, painted with a slur, hung with posters on which the slogan "Make America Great Again" had been altered to say "Make America White Again." The door to her college residence was vandalized too. Other Black students in the building woke to find their cars and doors vandalized. What could I conclude except that White students, her classmates and neighbors, had made note of who was Black: where they lived and what vehicles they drove. Otherwise how could vandals, if that's the word, have known which cars and doors to target. This inference might seem like overthinking it, but it was my first thought, the first thought mothers of my daughter's Black college friends had, too, that our children had been under surveillance.

One of my friends, who was White, said, "But your insurance will cover this, right?"

For a year, I'd watched as the candidate who eventually won had campaigned through small cities, hosting rallies where Blacks were shoved and punched. When I worried aloud about this trend to friends in my real and virtual neighborhoods, they sometimes said I was paying too much attention to far-off news. When I shared close-up bad news concerning my daughter, and at first it was just the hate activity vandalism, my real and virtual friends didn't know what to say. This went on more than a year. By the third year, aftermath in which safety seemed like a lost idea, what I said must have seemed connected to nothing the people I knew in my real and virtual neighborhoods understood.

Here are fact-checked facts about the incited violence at campaign rallies: In Cedar Rapids, Iowa, on February 1, 2016, the candidate said, "Knock the crap out of him. I promise you, I will pay for the legal fees." After a rally in Birmingham, Alabama, on November 21, 2015, "He should have been roughed up!" In Valdosta, Georgia, March 1, 2016, the candidate's security ejected Blacks from a rally as Whites shouted, "Go home, nigger."

At that time, journalists still called this unconcealed incitement "dog-whistle racism," as in dogs hear it and come running, and so, it follows, only racists hear it and come running. My daughter was born in 1997, when name-calling and insisting on certain spaces as White-only had diminished to the point that social scientists had begun to study, not explicit or violent racism, but those barely articulated prejudices by which, in the research of sociologist Eduardo Bonilla-Silva, White subjects describe themselves as not racist while using coded but belittling stereotypes, explaining their lack of interaction with people of color as "natural," everyone "naturally" preferring their own kind.

The year she was eighteen, however, explicit racism was on the upswing. Her property had been damaged. I hoped her corporeal self wouldn't be. I hoped her incorporeal self wouldn't be, but concern for that shifted to the backburner. Like the Ancient Mariner, who must have been good enough company once, I tried to tell people what happened. As more events transpired, friends or neighbors whose lives were proceeding as usual asked: "How are you?" They'd be en route to somewhere nice—like wedding guests on their way to the reception—and I detained them and recounted my news.

My brain was overfilled with it and leaking. The first bad news wasn't even the vandalism. That was three days after the election. Hours after the election, buildings at the university where I teach—which is not the college my daughter attended—were plastered with flyers we called "the racist flyers" because we thought they were a one-off. As more appeared, we called them "the hate flyers." When big posters sampled elements from Nazi propaganda on high-quality paper stock, with anti-Semitic slogans changed to anti-Black and anti-immigrant, we called them "the White supremacy posters" because they weren't anonymous anymore, but sponsored by an organization whose members photoshop their faces to a blur, the high-tech version of the hooded robe, in otherwise convivial-seeming group photos you'd find if you're masochistic enough to search the internet for information about the organization hanging expensive posters where you work.

Flyers and posters appeared again and again, always hung during the wee hours. I'd never seen or heard of any like them in the previous decades I'd taught. One night, a huge banner was hung across the multistory library. Patrols increased, but it's a big campus, and not until thirteen months later did campus police—with help from the FBI—catch the nonstudents hanging them, members of a national White supremacy group. They were charged with a misdemeanor, criminal trespass, because hate posters are free speech.

On the day the first of these appeared, the racist flyers we saw as an aberration, students arrived to class, stunned. A diminutive Mexican-American male—so disciplined and idealistic that, though professors aren't supposed to have favorite students, he was, I confess, easy to like, easy to teach—arrived late and out of breath. He'd been followed as he'd crossed campus, pushed and called names, by a guy with a torso painted to say "Daddy Won."

My daughter's car and residence door were vandalized the following night, and the next day, I filed a police report. The White and cheerful officer told me not to worry. His father had told him college kids went crazy for politics in the 1960s too. I wanted to explain that college kids in the 1960s went crazy agitating *for* civil rights, but I needed him to find us simpatico, not strident, and to increase patrols through the part of campus where my daughter's residence was. Two days later, Monday morning, I called the office of the college president at my daughter's school, hoping to ask her to issue a statement affirming the values found on the college's website. *Respect; Diversity; Collaboration; Innovation.*

An administrative aide answered the phone, sounding a bit like Ann Richards, former Texas governor renowned for feminism but also for her husky voice and countrified one-liners. The administrative aide told me the college president was in a meeting, but she'd be happy to help. What did my call concern? I described the vandalism and why I hoped to speak with the president. The administrative aide paused. Then laughed. *Softly or amusedly, with satisfaction.* That's the dictionary definition of "chuckle." It was six days after the election. The administrative aide was contentedly processing the fact her candidate had won, which perhaps surprised her as it had many. She said, "Honey, I assure you that won't happen. This office doesn't involve itself in politics."

I explained that my call wasn't political, that the college was funded to educate every student in good academic standing, and vandalism organized to intimidate one demographic contradicted the taxpayer mandate and the college's mission. Once my rhetoric changed from worried mother to informed citizen, she switched to a semblance of concern.

Soon, I started hearing from, and about, people with similar news.

Former students teaching at colleges and high schools across the state emailed me about incidents at their schools. One teaching at a high school in a San Antonio exurb wrote that students entered the classroom of another teacher, shouting for her to go back to Mexico. Never mind that families of the teacher had lived in the area for generations, no doubt longer than families of some students writing slurs and vague threats on the teacher's chalkboard. The teacher cried in front of her students, and the principal sent her home.

I contacted the *Texas Observer*, known for its investigative journalism, and a reporter started an online "Hate Watch" list, using contact information from my former students to fact-check incidents that became the list's first entries. The list grew longer, hate incidents proliferating. I emailed national newspapers, not describing vandalism directed at Black students at my daughter's college because the fact-checked date, time, location, and cell phone pictures of her car and residence door could make her a future target. I described the posters and incidents at the university where I teach, supplying dates, times, locations, and cell phone pictures. I described posters and incidents I'd heard about from colleagues at universities across the country, who'd supplied dates, times, locations, and cell phone pictures. One newspaper, the *Washington Post*, ran the first story. Other newspapers followed suit, reporting incidents I'd heard about and more. I kept reading as accounts appeared, hate incidents proliferating, and perhaps I was too informed.

I read the comments. Not under news stories but in threads under links to stories I posted on social media that got shared. Because social media organizes your feed according to your politics and ideology, I encountered people who concur in theory but disagree in nuance. I noticed that some found the hate activity shocking in a not entirely unpleasant, horror-flick way: revulsion mixed with thrill. Others read the accounts, then wished they hadn't. I get it. If I could have unlearned it and stayed alert to danger, I would have. A friend of a friend called the hate activity "unfortunate." I appreciate this word's emphasis on fortune, which creates and destroys happiness. Though hate activity is unfortunate, she commented, we should ignore it. "No one's in danger. Sticks and stones!"

I replied that vandalism telling minorities to go away (go where?) sounds like a threat, and as the mother of a college student who'd been targeted I felt she was less safe than she'd been a year earlier, and she couldn't stop going outside, not without stopping her life. And sunset happens earlier in winter, I added. My aside about sunset was odd, mealy-mouthed. But, as the sun sank, I was far from my daughter. Everyone gets anxious after dark.

The woman kept on, generalized opinions. A man I also didn't know told her to remember she was responding to a real person, not to her phone or computer, to summon manners, empathy. She told him, not me, that people like me were too afraid of death, and we should realize that our child can die anytime for any reason, e.g., slipping in a bathtub.

My stepson once said, precociously, when he was young: "The internet is mean, Debra. Everyone knows that." Years earlier, a friend, a psychologist, had remarked that social media made the net of connection broad but perilously thin. My husband, who has a deeply ingrained sense of privacy, has always wondered why a plate of paella or someone's new shoes are worth broadcasting. Before Facebook—which I'd first joined to understand it so I could make rules about it for my daughter, who was then in middle school—my husband had wondered at the logic behind Christmas letters, private recitations to diffuse audiences about band concerts, soccer games, family vacations, promotions.

After the "people should realize their child could die" comment, I tried to avoid the subject, but I'd scroll for news about who got married or had a new job and stumble across a post that hit close to home and find myself venturing out again, offering that I was in an interracial family and not just generally uneasy, that a specific this or this happened in my real, not-virtual life, in my child's real, not-virtual, life. One day, I read a post from a White woman in California—someone I didn't know whose friend-request I'd likely accepted because we had hundreds of mutual friends—calling for blue-voting states to secede. It was pointless to tell her red states had diverse regions and vulnerable people would get stranded, but I did, and she replied that a civil war was coming, and that many minorities would unfortunately suffer and die for a better future. I logged off. I left social media, my virtual neighborhood that was sometimes mean, the connections I was making perilously attenuated, because its diffuse audience was off-target for my private truth.

Meanwhile, a trifling real-life problem derailed me. My daughter's car developed an electrical short and would lose power as unpredictably as it would restart hours or minutes later. I hated that it kept restarting because no mechanic can fix an electrical short until the car stops for good, forever. When she drove home one weekend, it stalled in a rundown town I'd noticed as we passed through on the day we'd first moved her to college.

And, no, I didn't foresee that I was sending her into a hotbed, as the husband of my real-life friend later suggested I should have foreseen, small talk across a restaurant table on his wife's birthday. Foreseen how? Researching, I'd found that the town and college had a bigger Black population than Austin did, which seemed beneficial. At the start of her first semester, before the election then, when most people still thought the candidate who *wasn't* hosting violent rallies would win, we drove my daughter to college and on the way passed through an even smaller town with confederate flags. I typed this town's name in my phone and read about its history as a "sundown town," an all-White municipality that, as late as 1966, enacted violence to force "coloreds" to leave before nightfall.

It was forty-some years later and after nightfall when my daughter, on her way home, broke down there. She phoned. She'd called Triple A, but a tow truck wouldn't arrive for hours. Later, my husband said he'd down-played his fears that night, hoping not to heighten mine. I phoned my husband's cousin, a retired schoolteacher who lives twenty miles from where my daughter was stalled. She said, "It's not safe now, no. We live out here and hear what people say. We're heading over to wait with her until the tow truck shows up." Then my daughter called back. Her car had restarted. My husband and I waited out the next two hours—watching TV, our verisimilitude of composure—until she arrived.

At the neighborhood car dealership the next day, I told the service manager that not taking action until my daughter's car broke all the way down would be fine if she lived near and we could pick her up, but she was away at college, getting stranded. The second time I said this, I pointed at her through glass, in the hall outside the service manager's office, her beautiful corporeal self. Her incorporeal self? She now won't talk about any of this. But if I had to guess about that day and that time, when so far only the vandalism had happened, she probably thought, as I still hoped, that the vandalism was a one-off. The service manager said I should buy another car. I said, "Right now?" This dealership includes in its adver-tising its practice of hiring women and minorities, good marketing in a progressive city. The service manager was a White woman. I lowered my voice: "You see the dent and traces of paint? Someone hammered her car and then painted it with racist names and slogans. When she breaks down, my husband and I get worried."

"Talk like that wouldn't bother me," the service manager said. "I grew up with it."

"It's directed at my daughter," I said. "That's different."

The service manager's desk chair squeaked, rolling. Perhaps she was genuinely casting about and helping me to problem-solve. Or not. She said, "Maybe pull her out of college?"

My daughter didn't want to quit college, and I didn't want that. As her car kept breaking down, I reminded myself that a breaking-down car isn't a threat, just recurring vulnerability to a threat, and I tried to get it fixed, even as mechanics said it couldn't be until it died for good. But I couldn't relax, so I tried new mechanics, two in her college town, no dice, then drove over and traded her car for mine and drove a rental car while getting her car fixed in Austin with a mechanic who swore he could fix it, then felt sure he had, having taken the car apart to examine every connection, all of which was cheaper than buying another car, but not cheap, and I called her to come and get her car, which broke down when she was miles away. I bought another car, which seemed like a solution.

Conversations on my real porch. We'd lived in our big house for ten years and would soon follow through on a long-standing plan to move to a smaller one since both kids had left home. Over the years, neighbors sometimes walked over as my stepson might play his ukulele on the porch, or my daughter perfected her cheerleading handsprings on the lawn, or one of them posed for photos for prom, or stood in front of their packed car while leaving home for college. My daughter had some neighbors' spare keys because, when they'd traveled, she'd tended their pets.

A well-traveled neighbor with many pets who self-describes as "an old liberal" asked me how my daughter was enjoying college. My daughter was still a freshman at the little college then, so after the vandalism, after the car's breakdown and replacement. She'd also been called Jim Crow–era slurs from afar. Students seemed to socially self-segregate there, which might be usual, I speculated: the region's demographics, its entrenched customs. At home, she'd had Black, White, and Latina friends, maybe because the Black population in Austin is small. This is what I was going on about to the neighbor.

She shook her head. "Everyone's only been friendly to me in that town." I said I'd felt that too, but as White women, she and I were treated differently. I asked if she knew that the racial climate on many campuses was volatile. Not only had the university where I teach been in the news for hate activity, so had her alma mater a few blocks away. What did she say? "A few people are racist, but you can't be so thin-skinned." I decided

not to tell her, as I'd told the "sticks and stones" and "people should realize their child could die in a bathtub" woman, as I'd told the car dealership
service manager, that hate-speech-as-hate-vandalism feels like a threat.
And who's to say it's not? Not everyone who uses hate speech commits
a hate crime, but common sense tells you everyone who commits a hate
crime uses hate speech.

Another neighbor had a porch near mine and a daughter in high
school. When I told her my daughter's car and residence had been vandalized, her eyes widened. "We all feel so mother-bear when our child is
bullied for having curly hair or being a science nerd, but that is worse. I'd
worry it could escalate." It hadn't yet, not yet. We talked next about her
political concerns I theoretically share. And I cared viscerally, as a mother,
that her daughter had been shunned by friends whose parents had voted
differently in the 2016 election than my neighbor did. Then, when the
next round of posters appeared on my campus, the neo-Nazi ones, I worried aloud in front of this neighbor that the poster hangers seemed so
well-funded, so well-organized, so national, and where would it all end?
She said, "Hey. I want to mother your mothering here. You think about
race too much. You need to stop. Because if you do, your daughter will.
That's a big burden you put on her."

My brain and mouth felt out-of-sync as I said my daughter and I mostly
talk about her friends, professors, homework, but we talk about racism
when something bad has happened. I'd spoken expansively to my neighbor because I wasn't worried about scaring her. I never spoke expansively
to my daughter, whom I tried not to scare. I described some fears to my
husband but—as any couple passing through a hard time does—we orbited
in for essential exchanges, then back out to easier subjects. I'd put the burden not on my family but on neighbors, service managers, and strangers,
with my unprompted overflow.

I guess I thought it was my duty because of that adage about good people and the existence of evil. Or I wanted to make hate activity communi-
cable. Or I was crowd-sourcing my trouble, hoping that someone in the

unlucky horde I'd detained might know, not just that the news was bad, but how I might get back into my life and how I might get my daughter back into hers. Yet she'd just left home. So back into what we'd thought it would be as she'd taken SATs, shopped for dorm supplies, came of age, and drove away.

Another friend, good-natured, ironic, her hand on my shoulder, "No one's going to lynch her."

Six months later, my daughter was walking into her job at a grocery store in the midsized college city to which she'd moved for her sophomore year—a city with a bigger university and an international student body, all of which we'd hoped would make her safer—and she saw a group of White college students rushing at a group of Black students, yelling: "Niggers hanging around stealing cars!" A bad fight followed. Security camera coverage was video, not audio, and police took her name as the only audio witness to testify about hate speech before the fight, which, as free speech, isn't illegal. But testimony about it might mitigate punishment for the Black students, who'd fought back.

Less than a month later, and this is a completely unrelated incident, she was assaulted outside her apartment. Her assailant, her neighbor who'd harassed her for months, her neighbor I'd encountered while visiting, her neighbor I'd heard about again and again by phone, and I told my daughter to avoid contact with this neighbor when possible, was arrested, bond set high. Even I, with my temporarily waylaid sense of privacy, won't put into words here what happened. Because it's my daughter's story to tell, not mine. Mine is how—exposed to fear, growing habituated—I told the wrong people and stopped.

As planned, we moved. I soon came to understand the social intricacies of a cul-de-sac on the city's edge: no porches, just backyard decks behind privacy fences. One day, I heard what I thought was a domestic disturbance. I opened the back door to listen and heard, above a murmuring group, one man shouting: "Fuck Black people! Fuck Black people!" Giving all benefit of the doubt to the neighbors I heard but didn't see, he might have been their guest and not them. I did hear a woman trying to temper what he was yelling. But by then I'd retreated so far into private dread, into impatience with my dread, I thought that even if the man was my enemy he might be like me in one way—exhausted by rekindled racial hatred that won't be contained soon, though his rationale for containing it is vilely antithetical to mine. But hoping he wasn't terrifying was just hope, eternal.

On January 29, 2018, the *Texas Observer* broke a story revealing that most hate activity on campuses nationwide, the majority which targeted the university where I teach, was masterminded by a nineteen-year-old living in a Dallas suburb, and on August 12, 2017, one of his partners had driven a car into counterprotesters at the Unite the Right rally in Charlottesville, Virginia. On October 19, 2017, three more of his partners were arrested for attempted murder at a White supremacy rally at the University of Florida. It took days for me see that this news, anonymity ripped away, was more good than bad, that the ability of a bigot the same age as my daughter to marshal a handful of violent bigots was curtailed. Yet, perhaps because the backyard shouting had happened near my kitchen, my bedroom, my family room, my safe haven, my home, after I heard a faceless neighbor or faceless neighbor's faceless guest screaming his free speech behind a privacy fence, it took me longer to realize he probably wouldn't climb over the fence and hurt someone.

One morning in my bedroom, twenty feet from the privacy fence, I was dreaming I was talking with another newspaper reporter, still talking about hate activity, but we paused and smiled because somewhere an orchestra was tuning up, clusters of musicians playing riffs, phrases, lush music about to start. Then I woke. Despite the milk-colored sky, which usually seems sad to me because I like my skies sunny and blue, for the first time in months a branch draped against it seemed draped for effect, draped as if for my pleasure that has nothing to do with being stuck in a moment in history, or comments, or useless conversation. Pleasure arrived in one of those quiet moments I used to sometimes fill with trivial worry, yet none of this was trivial, though I'd compounded it, trying to confide.

It took me a long time to stop letting it slip in public. The person I'd accidentally detain would look bamboozled—*wait, what?*—maybe thinking what I'd mentioned was so strange that I surely caused or exaggerated it. But once in a while, someone asked for details and said back: Man, that's a lot. Or: You handled that better than many people. Or: I watched you freak out and settle in and deal, which helps me understand one day I'll do the same for different reasons. Or: I worry you're isolated. But only in isolation did I sense violins tuning up, flutes and woodwinds testing possibility, the sun pressing against clouds, and remember that joy—which even in good times lasts just hours or days—was dormant. Only in isolation did I pretend that comity in the neighborhood and everywhere was dormant, stirring. I stopped living on porches, real and virtual. I came inside.

3

Last Home

I'd take my father's fishing boat across the lake, down a creek, to other lakes, a chain of lakes. Then I'd cut the motor and drift to study cabins, most of them owned by people with year-round houses like the one in a nearby small town where I lived in winter. Lush grass extended to shorelines. Lake weeds swayed. For two months, the sun shone, intricate bugs shimmered, and my body felt interchangeable with air. I'd dip my hand in water and watch fish investigate its white flickering at the lake's surface, the fish's ceiling. I'd ignore a gaudy boathouse or striped beach umbrella—incongruous in that landscape of green trees, gray stones, opalescent water, and silver piers that seemed like sidewalks leading to doors. Some cabins had names. Tanglewood. Shangri-la. Cloud Nine.

Our cabin was filled with curious old furniture, bed linens, oddball kitchenware. We'd bought it furnished when its owner died. Mauve—for chairs, lamps, vases—had been a popular color. In the shed, I found paint cans with labels that read "Rugosa Rose." Our lake had taverns with docks where my parents tethered their boat and went inside to drink while I ran to swings in big trees or wandered the edges of forest as fireflies blinked. Some days, motoring across wide water, I turned on my dad's gadget, The Depth Finder, to learn the lake. In one spot, the depth plunged to eighty feet. In the middle of the lake, I found a plateau, and I'd get out of the boat to wade, waving at people on shore, hoping to startle them by almost walking on water. Once, in a cove fringed by tall pines, I dove out of the boat to swim, and a fish as big as I was, a muskellunge, flashed by in the deep.

By day, I wanted to go far and wide, at least across the lake and down the creek. But at night, wrapped in a mauve blanket, dropping off to sleep, I'd scare myself awake. Maybe I'd steered the boat into brisk waves at steep angles, the hull making choppy warning noises as I hit surges that, mismanaged, would have flipped the boat and I'd have floated or sunk. Or maybe I'd treaded unknowable water. I was a daredevil in the daytime.

At night, the lakebed seemed like my deathbed.

Still, every morning I'd want back outside: wilderness rising up around me, my own.

Strictly speaking, it's not nature if I've arranged it with my perspective, finding landmarks, placing rocks and branches in sand or soil, making outdoor rooms. Or, after I grew up, planting borders and trellises to mark the edges of lots I own. But when I was a girl, I thought lakes and trees and birds and fish and sky were mine and I was theirs. Then I'd come back inside to civilizing conversations at the family dinner table and, in the autumn, when geese headed south, when grownups put on waders to dismantle piers and move them ashore so winter ice wouldn't crush them, back into town, back to school with its complicated strictures and fiefdoms. Contentment—whether sunlit or misty or magisterially somber under cloud cover, every familiar color deepening and lustrous—lasted for single moments or hours or, when I was perfectly unscheduled and lucky, entire days.

Recently, I made two lists with the idea I might use them to visit a goal-oriented psychiatrist recommended by a friend who'd developed acute postnatal anxiety. According to medical classifications, she'd been a "geriatric mother," or young enough to give birth to a child but old enough that, in her case, her sleep-deprived body had produced unhelpful hormones. I, on the other hand, am merely old, though not yet geriatric. Whenever my age gets mentioned as it pertains to a situation at hand, friends or colleagues, or maybe a ticket-taker adding a senior citizen discount, rush to say: oh but you could be in your fifties! One flatterer insisted that I could be in my forties. People deflect mentions of my real age because we all know that aging leads to irrelevance then death.

I've had my own surges of unhelpful hormones. Adrenaline swells.

Yet it seems to have always swelled. By now, I see my body as a container for memories of experiences I'd have preferred to avoid in the first place, so memories I'd like to delete—some violent, some intimating violence, some life-changing, some intimating unsettling life changes—and the container seems nearly full, just a few inches left.

I stopped sleeping.

Sleeplessness compounds itself, then magnifies fear, fear-fog blurring life's outlines. Then hope, belief in improvements pending, goes missing. Whenever I'd stopped sleeping in the past, I relied on busyness. I earned degrees that led to better jobs. I added onto a house—built half a house—working alongside my carpenters, electricians, and plumbers who bid low, worked shoddy, and required hypervigilant oversight. I wrote books, planted gardens, moved rocks into retaining walls, tackled stacks of paperwork. Project completion is distraction. Distraction is analgesic: symptoms relieved and root causes unaddressed. If the project involves physical labor, your body relents and lets you sleep.

Bonus effect, months later you have a new line on a resume, better living space, organized files, a book with your name on its spine. Meanwhile, the idea that the project requiring every thought, muscle, and iota of resolve will ward off future reasons for worry is placebo-like. Even if you don't trust Robert Frost's idea that the best way out is through, which implies you're stalled but aimed forward, not believing in somewhere else is bleak.

This time I couldn't locate a new rationale for busyness.

One list for a psychiatrist—years made into phrases—would be my neuro-relevant history.

The other list would be real and recent reasons for worry.

Lists might help a psychiatrist work more quickly, I felt.

Because who has much time?

I left intermittent paradise behind when I moved to attend college in a small city. My parents divorced and sold the cabin, not that as a young woman curious about my future I would have stayed so absorbed by local lakes, creeks, swamp, shore, firmament. Yet so far I hadn't liked "town," so at college I scuttled between my dorm room, classes, and dining hall, no eye contact. When other students went to the library, the sandwich shop, the beer joint, the gym ("it's *relaxing*," someone explained), I walked off-campus. I studied three-story houses with cupolas and multiple porches built in the early twentieth century by lumber barons and the merchants who'd served them; trim bungalows that looked like stage sets for black-and-white movies; stolid houses with big porches and leaded glass windowpanes; and off-kilter, shingle-covered boxes at the edge of town. On short winter days, when the sun moved below the horizon, lights came on inside and windows cast golden parallelograms onto the snow. I gazed indoors at the wallpaper, curtains, edges of upholstery, and at flashing silhouettes of people settling down for the night.

I used to think gazing inside meant I wanted a home for myself.

But I gazed after my own windows cast light, after I lived behind them with people I love, my husband, daughter, my stepson, one of us hanging up a coat, setting the table.

In my twenties, I gazed into other people's homes too long after dark because my own home was unsafe, occupied by a volatile ex-husband I was figuring out how to leave. My route sometimes wound back before he was asleep, and I kept walking while looking inside. From outside and lit up—though I was unhappy in it, each day a puzzle to be solved, each conversation a looming menace—my domestic inland looked idyllic. A creaky floor lamp cast a hazy glow over otherwise shabby armchairs encircling the fireplace, and my ex-husband, sequestered in back, watching action movies, pleasingly erased.

Around this time, I imagined I was a poet. A line that came to me all at once, a line that seemed right, was this: "If it happened once, it's a lie." It seemed like life's great truth, but when I tried explaining it to my writing teacher, he said it didn't make sense, that many true things happen over and over. Pressed to explain what I thought I meant, I couldn't.

I might have meant love. Love must present itself in new ways for me to believe it.

I might have meant that a workable life plan was one that hadn't failed yet.

At the time, if a house had happened to me once—by chance I'd occupied it, claimed it, left it—there'd be more houses and better houses because they'd be future houses.

I've lived in six states, eight cities, at two dozen addresses, and I dream about finding secret rooms in my former homes. Once, I opened a door leading to a twinned, second apartment, big, empty, another new start. These homes were records of how I'd accepted what was and then repaired or added on or renovated according to what I could contrive. In one dream, I've been too careless, too carefree, and someone has knocked down walls, trespassed with crowbars. Rooms in these homes merge with rooms in my current home, and I see people I used to know, faces, clothes, hairstyles from a bygone era. I'd once struggled to answer people who'd politely asked what these men I used to know did for a living. *Living off me. Sinking in debt. Spending my money. Making illegal deals.*

In one dream, in which past and present fuse, men sit in a row on my sofa. My worst stepfather is there, too, tilting on one of my dining room chairs, the look on his face daring me to contradict him. I spent years studying these men, anticipating their moods, hoping to placate. They eye my rooms, better than any of us had back then, pieces of new furniture mixed with the best of my thrift store finds, and I introduce them to my husband because my current home is our shared home. They take surly notice of my husband's courteous ways, his interesting face, the bits of evidence that he's good, not to mention solvent. He shakes everyone's hand, says pleased-to-meet-you. Then takes me aside to say he hopes they'll leave because they'll be hard to explain when the kids get home from school.

After I'd been married to one of these men, and before I married another, I lived alone in an apartment above an old store, in what used to be shopkeeper's quarters, big rooms, each one heated with a match-lit stove. I was on the lam from a bad apartment in town where I'd lived above drug dealers who'd played loud music every night, and I couldn't sleep. I became a silence-fetishist. From the windows of the new apartment, I stared at silent wheat fields that by midsummer were a windswept yellow ocean, by fall a shorn panorama, by winter an undulating field of white. Inside, I used every shop class skill and hopeful whim to revamp, to move the line of vision here, not there, because living with imperfection means a trick of the eye that edits, improves. I sheltered there for years.

Once, I lived in a jerry-built apartment in an old house, my bed with its bird-pattern bedspread fitted into a breakfast nook with an arched doorway across which I'd draped a gauze curtain. I loved my time there, even during a month when the next-door apartment was rented to a drunk who sat by his door half-naked and cursing, until he made a liquor store run, smashed cars, and police hauled him away; even during a month when pipes to the house broke, and I leapt across the boggy yard with a towel and soap to a neighbor's across the street to shower there; even though the olive-green shag carpet clashed with mauve knickknacks I'd amassed to match a mauve sofa I'd brought from the cabin.

Once, I lived in the middle of weeds and woods in a dank house built in the 1970s by a libertarian DIYer who'd believed worst-case predictions about the energy crisis, and he'd put cheap paneling in "the great room"—this is realtor-code for a room that serves as both kitchen and living room—and in a narrow hallway, where the cheap paneling buckled, excess insulation. I painted everything a color named Dream Light, and I tamed weeds. Rooms gleamed. Moonlight woke me, and I'd wander the yard at night, where white flowers gleamed. I lived in the center of my preferred and amended shapes and colors.

Later, I moved to the fastest-growing city in America to be with my husband, who lived there with his son in what once was a small house in a working-class neighborhood, but the expensive city grew, and the house grew. Our iteration—a renovation for our blended family—would be its fifth, the one to complete and harmonize the previous. "Is this old or new?" someone asked a few years later, walking through our commodious home.

Daylight shone into every room and—one of the house's best effects—through leaves on a banana tree near the dining room, spackling the walls in green-tinted shadow. Halls and short flights of stairs led to surprise alcoves. On the ceiling of a narrow passage, a skylight snapshotted the changing sky. Our children, adolescents becoming adults, sometimes left me droll notes on the kitchen counter. When my husband texted them that dinner was ready, they thundered downstairs, hungry, spilling news of the day. Once, walking in the neighborhood, I rounded a corner and a handsome man on a bicycle called out, and my heart thrilled involuntarily before I quite realized he was my husband. When my father-in-law came to dinner, we'd carry him in, his wheelchair too, and stream Czech polkas as he sipped beer from shorty bottles. My father-in-law died. The kids grew up.

Then the house was big. We discussed moving. I pictured a newly-wed cottage in which to recoup lost or suspended time, the initial besotted weeks when we'd managed four dates before we'd brought along the kids. My husband pictured the tidy house he wished his father had moved to before he got sick. We ventured forth, home-hunters. This is the first scaling-down, downsizing, which, people insist, is not another word for loss.

Two lists for the goal-oriented psychiatrist

One, my neuro-relevant history:

A sometimes frantic childhood. A sometimes violent early adulthood. Years of surviving on what I could earn or, when I was with my ex-husbands, earn plus borrow, or, after I left them, earn minus debt I was paying back, budgets so contingent that any unforeseen outlay—parts and labor for a car, a medical bill, a plumbing repair—required an iffy new budget to keep my home a gracious shelter from distressing possibilities pressing in.

Last, but persistent, oversensitivity to loud noises like drunk men yelling. It's irrational, but I can't help what memories of stimuli my hippocampus retains. Also secondhand loud music, bass line minus melody. I might be hardwired to hate this. I might hate it because of that longago year I lived above drug dealers, their bass line minus melody arriving through heat ducts shaking the imitation-brass bed in which I lay awake. I'd go downstairs, knock on the drug dealers' door, and they'd turn down music long enough to laugh at how unexpected and negligible I looked, knocking while wearing a winter coat over my nightgown, my face arranged into conciliation and hope. My heart races.

Two, some recent reasons for worry:

Though my husband and I moved to a perfect-sized house with tall windows that make some rooms into radiant chapels, a yard with majestic trees and also boulders with indentations that I filled with soil and planted with flowers, and we moved without movers, the two of us carrying boxes, chairs, beds, tables, disassembling a nine-hundred-pound futon frame to carry pieces inside to reassemble because we like projects, problems to solve, and though we had the advice of a famous realtor who always sold my husband's previous homes, and though this was a city where houses sell as soon as they're listed, our lovely old house with the flickering banana tree leaves inexplicably did not sell for months.

Months and months, no big deal. But these were also the months doctors said my husband had incurable cancer and ordered a scan, and I rejoiced at cancer-free results until I understood they'd ordered more scans, which were cancer-free too. But he stayed mysteriously sick. One doctor noted that a medication my husband took months earlier can, in rare cases, cause a rare illness, which he recovered from, months turning into a year during which he slept in a chair I'd reupholstered in gold-flecked fabric in a once-cheerless room I'd repainted. Then, without warning, he lost most of his hearing. Next, he awoke one day and saw only darkness punctuated by bright arch-shapes, light from elegant arch-shaped windows in our home (downsizing without loss a problem I'd solved). He had surgeries, then injections that turned his eyes blood-red, and his vision improved.

I wear earplugs in bed at night to drown out noise. Some days I leave them in and go outside to garden. My husband comes too. From what I can tell while listening and lipreading, we hear each other the same if I wear earplugs while he wears hearing aids. This feels intimate, all others' noise muted. Leaf blowers. Shouters. Shrieking children, a happy sound. I also can't hear birdsong or wind in grasses. One day, I asked him if, in a few years, when proximity to my job won't matter but proximity to hospitals might, we'll move again. We sometimes drive through the country, where house after house looks like home in the future-perfect tense. Home in the past is what I found and improved, haphazardness converted into intention. Home in the future is revived faith in better luck ahead.

Sometimes, I wake in the morning, grateful I've slept.

At night, I lay in bed next to my husband, our bed a sleep-raft on wide water, and I'm floating, floating, everything beyond or above that might crush us passing me by, trees, firmament, the water below and the sky above forever unknowable, the lakes and trees and birds and fish—the sky is my ceiling—visible for now. And I'm becoming theirs, theirs.

I drive home from work on country roads at night, black highways with one or two remote lights beckoning, and the world once again seems bigger, some of it surely mine if I arrange my place. But after all the work and optimism, what the luckiest of us will get in the end, and I've been lucky, is not the world but space inside four walls. In time, one-story, no stairs to manage. Then smaller, assisted living. Then smaller, your hospital room. Then the smallest. Drowsy, wrapped in a mauve blanket, I scare myself awake.

Through the Bathroom Window at Dusk

During a recent spate of bad luck, I waited for not-yet-detectable good luck to follow. I didn't renounce aggressive problem-solving either. People who've seen my problem-solving are sometimes startled, not by the results I get, apparently unsolvable problems sometimes improved upon, sometimes solved, but by how, as I assess and take aim, my problem-solving looks like neurosis. I study every newly detected facet for a new angle of approach, a peculiar angle, and my stabs at solutions seem desperate. Is this surprising? With all the changes piling up, I was entering something like a new developmental stage, one for a woman turning sixty, however, so, unlike developmental stages outlined in *What to Expect: The Toddler Years*, without the bulleted list of expected odd behaviors and ways to squelch them. My problems are as tangled as brain dendrites.

"Look," the anthropologist Melvin Konner wrote in *The Tangled Wing: Biological Constraints on the Human Spirit*, about photos taken with a microscope, "experience really does change the brain." I'll start with my oddest behaviors and work backward.

• Avoiding the South and West Sides of My House

People say about interiors of houses they like: the natural light! In November 2016, White supremacy posters appeared on the campus where I teach. On my daughter's campus, where she was a Black freshman, racist vandalism proliferated: damage and painted threats on Black students' cars and doors at their college residences. Then she witnessed an assault. Then she was assaulted. Wait, the sides of my house.

We moved in 2017. My husband and I always planned to move to a smaller house when our kids grew up. We could have stayed, insisting that my daughter move back into her childhood bedroom so I could forever monitor her excursions with the phone app Find My Friends to ascertain she was safe. But where was safe? She wanted to be a college student and I wanted that for her, adult life. I assumed, she assumed, and administrators assumed, that each racist incident would be the last, not another in a series of escalations. But a few years later I stopped believing in personal agency. Why had I ever? Who can fix much besides the kitchen sink? Now, south and west windows.

How salutary to shop for houses. New visions, new conduits for what people call nervous energy. The realtor showed me one on a city's-edge neighborhood my husband had vetoed in advance as too bland, I told the realtor, getting out of her car. She said: let's still look to get a clearer sense of your needs. Outside, in the yard, I shrugged. Bland yet magnificently shady. I went inside and noticed the light. I later told my husband he should see the house. A day later, in the yard, he shrugged: bland. But beautiful trees, he added. He went inside and noticed the light. He sat at a kitchen table in bay windows on the south side and said we should buy the house. Most rooms had floor-to-ceiling windows including on the south, the master bedroom, and the family room, the heart of the house. Two big bathroom windows faced south and west.

I left most windows without shades or blinds, including the kitchen and family room windows on the south side, for unimpeded views to the apse of sky, its fresco of branches, the carpet-like grasses rimmed by an uninspired privacy fence above which jutted what were still the innocuous backs of other houses. The big bedroom windows on the south side had thick indoor shutters. I put up blinds in the bathroom, south and west.

A few weeks after we moved in, on Labor Day 2017, I was slicing and stirring at the kitchen counter, ten feet from bay windows, appreciating light, and I heard a conspicuously belligerent bellower, a man, also a shrinking but valiant woman talking at the same time, her insistent monotone underneath his, like she was adding a conceding yet more tactfully expressed viewpoint onto the subject that first got him started.

I opened the back door, south side. The man was shouting, "Fuck Black people. Fuck Black people." Then I heard a third voice, another man's, also mollifying. Then the party resumed. My husband said that, despite the privacy fence, the neighbors' patio is too near our windows that let in light but also sound and that the neighbors are hateful but until they threaten us or exceed the city's noise ordinance nothing's actionable. I spent the rest of the night looking out windows at torsos flitting above the privacy fence. I went outside and, shrouded by darkness and leafy boughs, stood on the fence crossbeam, watching people in chairs on a patio viewing a TV affixed to a wall.

In the next months, my daughter witnessed the assault and was assaulted. My odd habits began. A few times, I thought our air conditioner starting up was the neighbors starting up. When I was outside in back planting or pruning and heard them, I'd yell make-believe gardening instructions to my husband who was inside or miles away on his bicycle. *Bring the hose*, I'd shout. *Do you have the rake? Get fertilizer from the shed.* Modeling better backyard discourse. Demonstrating that noise carries. Indoors, when my willpower lapsed, I held my ear against windows to check I heard nothing. I hid this behavior from my husband because if he didn't know maybe I wasn't doing it.

I gathered facts by accident. One day, I was in the bathroom and noted to the west—over the privacy fence because our bathroom is higher—a man bellowing and staggering near his swimming pool. One year after the first Labor Day event, on our second year in the house, this man caused a second Labor Day event. I hadn't yet surmised—and I'm not still sure because it was dark when I'd stood among leafy boughs on the first Labor Day to see the patio-sitters watching their big TV—that the pool-wanderer might be the racist bellower. A lot of people drink. Many are bigots. But a bellower is rare.

On the second Labor Day, then, we heard bellowing from the west. Later that night, we heard an amplified and crackly voice—a police officer's through a SWAT team megaphone. Over and over, the voice ordered the pool wanderer, holed up inside, to come out unarmed with his hands up. From my bathroom window, I watched red emergency lights swiping the night sky. A police car pulled up in our street. Two officers knocked on our front door and told us— our backyard is catty-corner—to stay away from windows. The next morning, my husband and I stood in the bathroom and watched the pool wanderer, Caucasian, silver haired, in a navy blue shirt, walking his yard.

He'd caused an armed standoff and was released as soon as he sobered up. Not everyone would have been. Anger starts in your midbrain and readies you for battle. Since most of us don't do battle around the house or yard, the midbrain is overruled by the prefrontal cortex, site of high-order impulse curbs. I wasn't afraid, due to my cerebral cortex, site of rational thought. People posting on the gossip-and-handyman-tips website Nextdoor reported he hadn't threatened a wide-scale rampage, only his wife.

I started giving those two sides of the property a wide berth.

I slept in the master bedroom with thick floor-to-ceiling window shutters shut. When the shutters were open, I admired the view from a few feet back. I kept the bathroom blinds half-mast. I sometimes didn't invite friends for dinner because I didn't want to enact the semblance of tête-à-tête while eating at the table near the bay windows.

• Beautifying a Mistake

My daughter told me about websites she'd consulted (7 Ways to Walk Safely, What You Need Walking Alone), the locks on her doors and windows, her pepper spray. She earned good grades and made good friends. Omitting violent disruptions—though violent disruptions are a lot to omit and yet she rebounded quickly, and I'd suggest therapy, and she'd decline—she was almost having the college experience I'd pictured.

I didn't hate the new house. I'd walk into a room and sigh at how vivid and graceful the shapes and colors in a well-lit room are. Inside, I sometimes heard birdsong. This forced a verdict. Do I enjoy birdsong? Or turn on music? If I can hear birds, I might hear a neighbor. After the patio neighbors' college-age son came home the next summer, I heard nearly constant electronic dance music until I climbed the fence crossbeam—neither parent in sight—and persuaded him I was a good person who couldn't wear earplugs so often.

Our previous house was still for sale, and I worked hard on that because, though I didn't reason this out at the time, moving away from the new house couldn't occur until the previous house sold, after which I'd explain to my husband that some houses on the planet are wrong. I won't list angles of approach that helped sell the other house, but I could write a website, 5 Tips To Sell Your House. Another problem I researched was how to make aural or visual barriers for the neighbors on the south and west sides. Soundproofing? Sheets of Styrofoam wedged in windows. Or maybe flesh-tone blinds you close by yanking chains and then ratchet onto woodwork with wingnuts.

I decided instead on visual barriers to avert my compulsive surveillance. Trees are expensive. Most are slow-growing. Yet the clerk at the nursery described some as good "neighbor-be-gone" varieties. I tell you this to emphasize that my problem is normal. I hired a crew to build and erect ten-foot-high trellises of varying widths and stagger them at artistic angles around the south perimeter. To void my husband's suggestion that I landscape only after the previous house sold, I took freelance gigs and taught more. While not racing to and from campus, grading, writing, I directed a crew, called nurseries to find forty-eight Star Jasmines. I dug holes, gently untangled tendrils, wove vines upward. Star Jasmine is evergreen and, in a few years, densely luxuriant.

When we got an offer on our previous house, I told my husband we'd need to move again. The neighborhood, I said, so bland. My husband was alarmed. I'd just built those trellises I'd defended as a necessary expense so we could focus on what was lush and fertile. I never said I needed them to keep from fixating on neighbors and failing to block at home what's beyond my problem-solving range. The Unite the Right rally ending in murder—"good people on both sides"—dominated headlines then. My daughter hadn't been the victim of a crime for months, but when she called, between the time I'd hear the ring until I heard her cheerful "hi Mom," my heartbeat faltered.

When my husband and I drove across the city for the real estate closing, where the realtor had minibottles of champagne, and I don't usually drink before breakfast, but I did, I asked, intoxicated while sleepy: "What's good advice for people who bought a house and aren't in a position to move, but it has problems that can't be solved?" The realtor smiled. "I say spend what you can to make it pleasant and realize no home is perfect."

Afterward, my husband took me to a restaurant. Having watched me finish my minibottle and reach for his, he thought I should eat. He looked handsome and happy, talking about the trips we'd take.

He said now that the coffers were full I should spend what I needed to solve the problem I'd been going on about during the closing.

I ordered expensive blinds I was told would mute noise, but don't, for family room windows and bay windows, the south. I planted four trees, two expensive, fast-growing, and emerald-colored cherry laurels for the last gap, so I no longer see the pool wanderer, the west. I also planted, for pure beauty's sake, two Mexican buckeye trees, with pink flowers in spring and green foliage in summer that turns yellow in autumn.

• Telling Everyone While Telling No One

Lifelong, in roughest patches, I've told my bad facts to others to strip bad facts of power. Telling was shock overflowing. Others have similar experiences, I believed; I want to pool our grief, its lessons. However, telling bad facts is inefficient research.

Most White people thought of hate activity as a headline if they thought of it at all, though it was a recurring headline by then. Researching it—no matter how I phrased my search, "hate activity," "hate crime," "White supremacy," "White nationalism," "increased membership in hate groups"—I found new reasons for fear. When people asked the pleasantry question, how was I?, I reported my most recent bad facts, out of context.

I talked fast, excessive detail. In 2018, my brother-in-law told someone in my family, who told me, that he—unlike her, she stipulated—didn't believe that what I said had happened. He said I was a bleeding heart who wanted attention. To be fair, he heard my news as trickled-down gossip, no corroborating facts. To be fair, nothing like it had happened to him, a White man in a midwestern hamlet.

Telling reporters was easier. From late 2016 to early 2018, I felt that if the public knew what happened on my campus, in my state, across the country, that at least the president of my university would issue a persuasive condemnation. I wasn't so deranged to think that the president of my country would. But I must have wanted that because one night I dreamed I was talking to the political consultant Kellyanne Conway, and in the dream, she said I'd never get taken seriously in D.C. until I had smoother hair, a Brazilian blowout. I awoke. At the time, only the vandalism, spray-painted hate speech, had happened to my daughter. We hadn't moved yet. I told my husband my dream by the door in the old house as he left for work. He could hear me in the dark as we hugged, no lipreading required yet. He said the vandalism was demoralizing but over.

I was good at writing to reporters with my striking subject headings, my succinct but damning emails, my attached cell phone photos of ever-evolving posters on my campus with increasingly expensive paper and graphics, then banners on buildings. I didn't tell reporters what happened to my daughter because I was guarding her safety. But I did file a report with the Southern Poverty Law Center, which monitors hate activity, and a reporter searching those files called me for a human interest story with a human interest photo. I knew that genre: sad, bamboozled humans, so interesting. I declined.

My daughter knew her bad facts and a few of mine, but it was wrong to tell her I was afraid as she insisted she wasn't. She'd grown easily upset at low-stakes junctures and uncharacteristically vulnerable to perceived slights. Once, when she visited us to see the new house, the yard, the trellises, I pointed out windows and said, "Those neighbors are racists or socialize with racists." She asked me how I knew. I told her. She shrugged. If you're thinking we aren't close, we're close enough I recognized her usual avoidant coping.

My husband knew some of my bad facts. I moved my lips slowly in good light with steady eye contact and avoided contractions. Three Tips for Living with Someone with Hearing Loss. I hadn't lost the habit of patter, one-time fuel of daily intimacy, but he couldn't hear any of it. I could hear myself, muttering and thinking aloud. I loathed the neighbors to the south who'd had the patio party with shouting, but three years had passed now. I loathed the neighbor to the west who'd required a SWAT team, but two years had passed. I didn't expect my husband to understand because I didn't.

Three years later, the summer of 2020, the pandemic, I set up a Scrabble game on the table in the kitchen bay windows looking out at graceful trees, the domed sky. We ate there only when I preemptively streamed classical music, though my husband complained that, for him now, streamed music is a hollow roar. I sorted tiles, planning my next play. Neighbors to the south came out on their patio. I recognized them behind my trellis: music-blasting son and dad. They shouted at the top of their lungs like racists or ordinary neighbors.

It's discouraging to realize your mind is racing for the wrong reasons. I've researched this, The Amygdala and Memory of Emotion. My husband asked me if I was okay. I enunciated carefully as I said that what I felt was irrational, but I'd come to associate those neighbor noises—he couldn't hear them so I pointed—with racist shouting we'd heard that first Labor Day when we'd moved in, while the worst events were happening to my daughter. I wasn't having full-blown panic, I said, but my brain felt so snarled I couldn't think. He nodded, then stood and carefully carried the Scrabble board, so it wouldn't tilt and lose tiles, to the dining room table on the east side of the house, and we finished our game.

I knew the noise-to-fear link my brain made was pointless. Did it help to know? Not yet, I thought in the summer of 2020. Every night, the twilight made the backyard more starkly beautiful, the luxuriant vines on my trellises more mysteriously dense. I first pulled down the blinds, the family room first, next the kitchen windows. Then the big shutters in the bedroom. In the bathroom, I paused before closing off the view to the west, the day's final light seeping through backlit and blurry cherry laurel trees, washing the sky above amber-pink, turning the former worst view in the house into a kitschy and sentimental painting.

The COVID Sunday Drives

1

My friend once saw wildflowers in an alley, and a purple string mop set out to dry, mop head up, seemed to her like wisteria—its dangling purple strings—but I always want roaming to transport me, and I hope to be alone with trees, to be *do not disturb* with trees, admiring their smallest, highest branches waggling, and I'd have noticed instead a cast-aside Gatorade bottle or plastic trash cans or broken lawn chairs, and here I am imagining interferences with my transcendence, and I wasn't in that alley. But if I had been, I'd have begrudged the human middens, human evidence, would have recalled not wisteria but a job I once had cleaning vacation cabins in which guests left messes, and by the time I mopped my way out the door, I was aggrieved, hoping that what came next was better.

2

I always called the order to shelter in place *lockdown*, quicker to remember and say, though my stepmother who uses quotation marks like others use <u>underlining</u>, for emphasis!, wrote a letter from Wisconsin to say her "lockdown" was "worse" since she was "trapped," not due to "COVID," which was "fake news," but because the house she shared with my father was a "prison." Meanwhile, my husband and I cleaned our house in Austin, Texas, on Easter Sunday, vacuuming, dusting, scrubbing, and we finished early and took the first of our Sunday drives through pandemic-empty streets to open land where cotton-puff clouds rolled, no smog, the car rocking in gusts as trees bowed and swayed.

My husband told me that over the next hill was a church he remembered from decades of bicycling, decades of muscles stretching and contracting, days, weeks, years, miles recorded in inky columns of notes on a wall in our garden shed, a church he'd bicycled past before the city got expensive, and people bought houses in what used to be country towns, which became exurbs, and commuters filled roads, too dangerous for bicycles then. But the roads were empty on COVID Easter, the only COVID Easter, we believed, lockdown soon to be over, we believed, as empty as when he'd bicycled them with their blind hills and curves but no traffic except a solitary truck or tractor, its driver nodding, a salute, before giving him room enough to ride, he said, as we crested the hill and saw the white clapboard crisp against a periwinkle sky, a tin-roofed steeple flashing silver.

I had on ragged jeans, a T-shirt streaked with dust and cleaning powder, my husband's sunglasses, mine on the desk where I'd left them a month earlier, and I stood on the church's porch, properly called a parvis, from the Middle English *parvys*, from Old French *parevis*, from Latin *paradīsus*, from Greek *parádeisos*, and maybe congregants earlier crossed it to sing and pray, thinking COVID was a city problem, or service got canceled but an impassioned flower-lover wanted the church bedecked all the same, because at the top of steep stairs on the parvis was a flower-cross as tall as me, a chicken-wire cruciform studded with flowers starting to wilt, and wind whipped my hair like banners, so it seems in a photo my husband took, and the cross quaked and petals scattered.

At home, I wandered nearby gullies and thickets in what used to be ranchland but got carved into lots for houses with acres saved for mostly empty trails through branches and mud, trails where I found a treehouse begun and abandoned by kids no doubt grown now, an occasional orange plastic tag marking someone else's progress. At first I had trouble finding my way in, and out, but learned to see veiled portals, to ignore the sound of the expressway, and if I walked far enough, past trees and boulders, past a stretched-out remnant of rusty wire attached to old posts, past a sprawling cactus into a meadow of tall weeds, I would hear just birds and wind, and once I ended on a highway on the edge of the city, stepping out of a tangle into light where people, after I rounded the corner to the sidewalk, stared. Because I had a too-private look on my face, having been recently ecstatic.

3

The ancients found the sublime in celestial bodies. The Romantics found it in remote vistas, inaccessible canyons, mountains, oceans. Then the external world got demystified and the inner world mystified, the self with its tricks and caprices a site of reverence, inciting a speculative new theory of self, a theology of self. Depth psychology didn't get invented overnight, but the sublime is now *deep inside* and has been for over a century.

I wanted to be deep outside. Arroyos, hummocks, groves, towering trees.

Branches flexed. Grasses draped. I found flowers I didn't yet know, widow's tears. I found summersweet, which I bumped against and blossoms released, aromatherapy. Humming insects made a sound like one of those spa sound-machines tuned to a channel maybe called "peacescape." I wasn't lost, though I'd find myself four miles from home.

COVID spring became COVID summer, and I recalled Easter, the mesmerizing wind and strange highway. Every Sunday, I decided, we'd pack surgical masks, hand sanitizer, silverware for carry-out meals, and drive. We couldn't escape the pandemic, nothing so bad since 1918. We couldn't escape the rest of the confounding muddle of history inside of which we'd found ourselves stalled. But we'd get respite by driving, looking out our car windows and stepping outside for a closer look while keeping our social distance. As a child in a backwater town, I'd roamed for better glimpses of moss, ferns, keyholes of sky through the small and highest branches waggling, and I still displace onto rural backdrops the desire to live as undisturbed as Thoreau, whose mother, FYI, delivered his meals and fresh laundry. Desire displaced, or projection, was described by Freud.

4

I wasn't fixated on the bucolic when I was living in it, taking for granted the sensorily curated world, a peacescape, lakes, fields, horizon, sights, sounds, smells, and textures. Yet conversation went badly. I tended to blurt something I'd discovered while reading. "Communism has good ideas badly delivered," I said in Phys Ed once, a fine fall day, tennis day. "I feel blithe," I said to a friend of my mother's I'd passed on the sidewalk, hurrying to my after-school job on a slushy-sunny early spring day after long winter.

I didn't yet understand I'd give up what I'd thought was the entire world: the pinging of frogs, heart-shaped or star-shaped or elliptical leaves in infinitely varied shades of green, sunbaked rocks, birch bark unraveling dry yet sticky in my hands, the stinging-wet smell of snow, honeysuckle tips melting sweet in my mouth. The collectively atomistic life and the local economy, requiring physical toil, regulated small talk. If I put into words a vagary, my unexpected thinking, someone might take me aside to tell me I was trying too hard to be different. The linguistic anthropologist Shirley Brice Heath found that most people become lifelong readers because a parent or parents modeled the habit. But the occasional "social isolate," she noted, relocates community, kith and kin, in books.

During COVID walking, I remembered how, in the very first novel that a thoughtful schoolteacher gave to me, the protagonist Heidi is rushed back to the Swiss Alps from a city where, because she couldn't hear wind in trees, her health has failed. I pause when I'm far enough from the sound of traffic and osmose this medicine, wind in trees.

As an adult, I settled twenty miles from my job at a university and two miles outside a village where the cost of living was low, and I consorted with birds, cicada, lightning bugs. When I went out at night, deer sometimes approached me. Then I became a single mother, my daughter the only Black child in a classroom or on the school bus, and adults and children on the playground pried or kept us at arm's length. When she was a baby, she looked only at my face or at the sky or tall trees or—wonderingly, her eyes focusing and startled—at the moon. We had to live somewhere differently imperfect, part-Eden minus the lush garden, where the majority-minority dominant loyalties, the tribal habitat, would be more cordial. Karl Marx left behind his village idiocy for London, preferring an array of people and ideas, outsiders absorbed, flourishing. After I fell in love with a man in a city, with a son, a good life underway, my daughter and I moved.

I live and will likely die without enough wind in trees, with solitude that ends at the house's edge, the property's edge, enforced by privacy blinds and privacy fences, anonymity in a crowd a consolation. The rural and urban divide, the never-the-twain-shall-meet divide, is a national and political problem and a private and personal problem, mine.

5

I projected comfort onto Comfort, population 3,350. We got there by crossing the escarpment and passing through Blanco's white stones and blue-green waters, past Sisterdale's shingle mill and vineyards, onto plains wide and high, toward the sky about which my neighbor Roy, when I lived in the country, used to say: "People think there's no scenery and I tell them, 'Stop looking down, man! You got to look up! Look at the sky!'" Hills, berms, cliffs, mounds, valleys are in the cloud-roiled sky, rocks and bleached grasses mere groundwork. We rolled across a series of hills then downward into Comfort.

History is written by winners, of course. Part of Comfort's was written by European arrivistes, Freethinkers who didn't build churches, just small Greek Revival civic necessities, using quarried stone: a school, a hotel, a store, a post office, a bank.

> The Confederate States of America imposed martial law
> due to these abolitionist Freethinkers' resistance to the
> Civil War. James Duff's Partisan Rangers killed some
> Freethinkers in battle, executing others. Two-thousand
> escaped, some never returning.

My smartphone said that. We drove through the town as I envisioned life before and after the war, preferring not to conjure what my phone called the Confederate sympathizers' reign of terror—inflicted on lives spilling out of these houses onto porches, into gardens, toward the town square. I approved these Freethinkers, their message. If I'd lived among them, I'd likely have believed what they believed due to social pressure, influence, having attuned my values to match. But if I'd lived among Confederate sympathizers, who can say.

In 2002, when the state erected a historical marker about Comfort's founders, citizens protested, circulating a petition: "No Monument to Atheists in Comfort!" That Sunday, as my husband and I turned toward home, soothed by green evidence of spring, vines cascading, the river cascading, we crossed a bridge and saw under it a crowd, not as big as crowds on Florida beaches that weekend during a COVID spike, but maybe fifty people clustered drinking beer, wearing bright swimsuits, no masks. All the downtown shops had been closed, governor's orders, except for the ice cream shop outside of which masked clerks served unmasked customers. We wore ours as we sidestepped them, warily regarded.

The next Sunday, we drove between wind-swept pastures to Serbin—the remains of a colony established by Wends, ethnic Slavs who'd objected to Frederick William III's Prussian Union of Churches, which meant communicants would ingest bread and wine as symbols, not as transubstantiated body and blood. Descendants emphasize religious freedom as the motive for emigration. Yet historians note that Wends had dire economic need. Serfdom ended in 1819, but land still belonged to former landlords, so Wends were receptive when an exhorting, firebrand preacher told them science was replacing religion. Startled by the long list of the dead, parents instantly childless, children instantly orphaned, my husband said: "The threat of starvation. Or you'd stay home, doctrine or no."

Soft rain fell as we sat in the original church, a dog-trot cabin. Then we walked through the cemetery. Gravestones absorb groundwater and soluble salts. Limestone is susceptible to surface loosening ("sugaring") and stains. We found the children's section, lichen-covered stones covered by rose bushes as big as trees, rows of infant graves a testament to the ruthless swath of disease before antibiotics. Wendish brides wore black to remind them of assured suffering ahead. Decades later, they were allowed to wear gray, then white. Wends ostensibly moved because of theological distinctions now lost in the mist of time. If they're known at all today, it's for their fall festival and ethnic food, noodles.

6

Every Sunday, I studied the muddle of history.

Science and antiscience factions: people wore masks in the city and didn't in the country. Protests as likely to have occurred a hundred years ago as now erupted in cities, including Austin, and White supremacists counterprotested. Placards dotted city lawns: "Black Lives Matter" (frequent) or "We ♥ the Police" (infrequent). City dwellers mostly endorsed one presidential candidate. In the country, eight-by-three-foot banners on barbwire and three-by-five-foot flags flying from poles in stake pockets on tailgates endorsed the other. We saw a barn painted with one candidate's name, painted the way barns used to be to say "Gold Medal Flour" or "Mail Pouch Tobacco." Ads on barns are prohibited since the 1965 Highway Beautification Act unless the ad is folk heritage, but rural barn-owners object to these rules for barns.

Memories of times I'd lived in the country, when it was still easy to ignore who'd voted for whom, overrode my recent memories, for instance that in 2016 my daughter left home for a college in a small town surrounded by fields and farms. She endured bias-motivated vandalism and finally an assault, hate crimes, which made the postelection uptick of verbal incivility in the small college town harder, incivility a minor affront compared to the rest, but cruel, as in two women—"with blue-gray, church-lady hair, Mom"—who told her to give them her table in a coffee shop. "Get used to it," one said. "A new broom sweeps clean." She lives near now and we try, albeit in different ways, to forget.

On Sundays, I let myself believe I'd moved away from a hushed landscape for my daughter's formative years and could still return. I'd look at a farmhouse with a porch, access to wind and sky. "I want that," I'd say. My husband didn't answer. He knows I moved to Austin—progressive but an ethnic monoculture—for a tolerant if not diverse school for my daughter, and because, back then, either he or I needed to commute, and it couldn't have been him since my stepson lived parttime with his mother. But after the kids grew up, I missed wandering while blithe, wandering in starlight or dew, and my husband said we'd move back if I must. I mustn't. I picture ordinary days in the country, but not holidays.

Imagine. I've bought groceries in a nearby small town to cook the family feast and maybe my daughter is on her way, driving, and I text her to stop for a last carton of milk or pound of flour or another package of wrapping paper. It's not likely she'd be assaulted again, yet low-grade worry that she will be remains. More likely, she'd be subjected to inhospitable stares. I'd have bartered away her sense of welcome for wind in trees.

7

One Sunday, my husband and I drove to Castroville, stucco houses crisscrossed with timbers hand-hewn by Alsatian immigrants after a long voyage. We sat in the park, pecan tree branches creaking, clematis and moonflower leaves stirring. The town was deserted except for White people going in restaurants, some wearing masks, thereby obeying the governor's then-order for partial reopening that stated restaurant customers wear masks until they're inside when—defying logic—they take them off, open their mouths, and dine. Brown and Black servers in masks carried cartons of food to cars.

Once, we drove through High Hill, Ellinger, Praha to see churches nestled in trees in summer light, but we couldn't go inside—tours canceled, COVID—to see walls painted by Czech immigrants in tromp l'oeil to simulate the carved medieval sanctuaries they'd left behind. At Queen Mother of the Holy Rosary & Saints Peter and Paul in Hostyn, we stood in an outdoor grotto, the horizon staggeringly beautiful, as if filtered for Instagram.

Another Sunday, we drove through Lampasas and San Saba where historical markers describe hangings and shoot-outs. Homemade signs dog-whistled: "Jobs Not Mobs." Though this is the West, not the South, Confederate flags flew next to MAGA flags. An unmasked man stared at my masked husband swiping his credit card at a gas pump, then walked antagonistically too near. I recalled an advice-column letter I'd read:

> Dear Amy,
> We have seen negative comments congregants have
> posted on Facebook, such as, "Wearing a face mask does
> not help," "Stop wearing underwear on your face," and,

from our minister, "If I see you wearing a face mask, I'll laugh at you." We are naturally uncomfortable.

And yet the next Sunday—fifth month in the year of our pandemic—we went for another drive.

Navasota was almost too far, but we'd passed through our same-old living room, kitchen, hallway, bedroom all week, so we drove, first to the edge of Austin, passing through neighborhoods where masked people hurried down crowded sidewalks. Then we drove through suburbs, exurbs, until the view got wider, panoramic, green cornfields tremoring, ready for harvest, the sky faded cobalt in midsummer heat. From behind the windshield, I watched fields of vision moving like on a streaming TV show my husband and I had discovered, a documentary we thought, but, no, a camera fixed to a boat lets viewers feel as if they're on a river, not urgently searching for new TV due to COVID lockdown.

Navasota is the South, not the West. Houses with historical registry plaques have sweeping porches, gingerbread, and turrets. Brick and stone buildings with iron trim line the downtown streets once so overrun with "ruffians" that White women and children were told "to stay inside." Tucked between buildings was a mural, Blues Alley, because music is the ethnic influence people like, no sectarian arguments there. I read my phone:

> The 1858 tax roll listed forty-two residents as holders of twenty or more slaves, the index of wealth often used to define a "planter." By 1860 there were 4,852 whites in the county and 5,468 slaves.

A historical commission website reprinted articles from the *Central Texian*, the town's first newspaper. January 24, 1857, "Slavery Agitation," the standard arguments: reports of mistreated slaves were essentially fake news; slaves were happy; outsiders interfered; God approved. February 14, 1857: "Perhaps you can spare able negroes to work on the road."

My husband and I stood on the sidewalk. Sun beat down.

Hypocognition is a term from linguistics that describes how concepts don't seem to exist if words to describe them don't exist. If a culture has no word for "grief," people might report "sickness" or "strangeness." The opposite is true. If you have words for a concept but no experiences to match, you might report skepticism. We have words for racism, discrimination, systemic oppression, bigotry. But whether someone who has no experience to match believes that these words describe reality depends on what else they've experienced, who they elected to trust, how tied they are to a like-minded own kind.

In the interest of middle ground, I sometimes try to grasp the refusal to know. All I can report firsthand is perhaps just an early evening in my front yard the year before my daughter was born. My father and stepmother had come for a visit and they'd spent the previous night in Tulsa, a nice city with nice people they said. The sun sank behind trees. Tulsa was in the news, the seventy-fifth anniversary of the 1921 Tulsa race massacre. The Oklahoma legislature had appointed a committee to make a historical record, to establish a probable body count, to search for mass graves. My dad, with his vague faith in experts but instinctive objection to history that isn't about the courage of great ancestors, winced. My stepmother said, "It's long ago. I don't know why anyone cares." I wondered whether to answer her. She turned and went inside. That day in Navasota, my husband and I went home.

8

We returned by a different route, through green glens and remnants of small towns, empty storefront buildings clustering then vanishing, then open land that looked familiar. We were near where my daughter went to college in 2016. How pretty it all seemed when we drove her for a college visit. A year later, after dire and also sometimes merely unpleasant events, my fond first impression had dissolved. Driving, my husband told me we'd run out of towns now. I was holding ice on my face—I'd stumbled over a carriage block while reading Navasota facts on my phone. Unmasked people had rushed to help me. My husband waved them away and assessed my injuries. "Nothing broken. Bad bruise. Split lip." In the car, we wondered what future escapes from lockdown would be.

The next Sunday, we didn't drive.

City parks with lakeshore, sculpture, or legendary views were too crowded. We picnicked in a nondescript pocket park built as a hedge against amassing noise, density, pollution, heat. The next day, while riding his bicycle on a shady street—random bad luck—my husband was hit by a car. In my kitchen, I held my phone, listening as the ER doctor finished an emergency intubation, then sent him to a trauma hospital. I heard her shouted instructions because the person who'd answered the phone forgot to put me on hold.

I don't remember days that week, my lockdown a <u>prison</u>. I remember nights. The moon waxed toward full as I lay on the floor to see above roofs of houses, above yard lights and streetlights—you've got to look up!—and I saw textured and phosphorescent clouds racing across the wide moon, and then the clouds would break, and the moon glimmered, a silver coin. In the valley of the backyard, rimmed by tall houses, I watered my plants in pots, midnight gardening, turning on the tap to listen for the whoosh of water rushing into pipes rhythmic, pinched, and squeaking, like maybe a snipe winnowing then singing.

9

After my husband came home, I studied photos I'd taken the spring before. A trail framed by graceful branches, trees with new buds silhouetted against a damp sky, a clump of red flowers, a spray of yellow—all timestamped at the start of the pandemic. Paradise means "near" or "around" (*para*) "god" (*dyēus*). With the country in lockdown, which is history, three-and-a-half years after the 2016 election, which is history, having seen my daughter's life changed in the years since, our family history, I'd walked trails to avoid thinking, willing away all human evidence because the worst human instincts had been inflamed.

I surrender to history. I miss sights and sounds from the other side and visit them as a tourist on Sunday drives. After youthful optimism, Herman Melville abandoned the idea that order and justice are achieved through willed human action and believed instead that survival is buoyancy and adaptation. "Let go and let God," a nineteenth-century, splintersect Methodist, a Keswickian, advised. "History is a nightmare," James Joyce wrote.

One day I hiked, not away from the city as I used to, but toward the city, through a deafening overpass, past a discarded cooler, past a smashed pallet flown off a truck, past swatches of winking and glittering trash, onto a flood plain never cleared or regrown, under a swaying canopy of trees, onto a mudcrack trail—mud tessellating into a mosaiced floor—and onto a footbridge. I gave myself over to a fallacy of bridges and decided to believe the bridge had been created just for me, also the stairstep rocks leading out of bottomland.

I walked further into sunlit and shadowy sights, whispering and trilling sounds, humid smells thickly fragrant, and I headed into trees, deep outside, came to a curve, headed back, and I heard the drone of traffic, shouts from a high school football practice on the other side of the creek— no peacescape without distraction. I was sharing the trail with a dog with a plumed tail, I thought. But, no, it was a fox, giving me a head-shaking glance.

My phone rang, and I answered it, standing on a path sprinkled with bright stones painted by children bored with lockdown—one red-and-black-dotted like a ladybug, one with an American flag, one orange with a school mascot, one blue with a butterfly. My daughter had called me, she said, because she was "flustered," a stopgap word she's used in recent years to describe her new surges of worry or dread over trifles, surges a helpful expert would call displaced panic. But my daughter so far will not.

She's fine, she insists from the hub of her unnamed grief, feeling sickness and strangeness, and then she talks in a jagged voice and breathes too rapidly, describing minor problems, and then she relaxes again.

This was days after the 2020 election, the vote count extending because of the hundreds of thousands of mail-in votes due to COVID, election officials laboriously opening envelopes, smoothing and scanning ballots, and the losing candidate hadn't conceded. Protesters on one side: *count every vote.* On the other: *stop counting votes now, while we're still ahead.* The week before, in the country, ten miles from my daughter's apartment, a convoy of pickups with armed drivers flying three-by-five-foot candidate-name flags in tailgate stake pockets had forced a campaign bus for the winning candidate off the road. She'd heard about it on Twitter, she said, inexplicably refusing to feel flustered about that. Twitter is bad news, BTW, not birdsong.

We said goodbye, and I headed home.

When options narrow, people who have freedom and opportunity migrate. I had to believe in somewhere. I had to believe in a place with less to fear, with more witnesses and more allied help when sectarian loyalty turns ugly, but no guarantees, the city a partial answer to an unsolvable problem. I arrived here, with parks and trails, with my daughter near, and, according to precinct data on my smartphone, a 72 percent majority of neighbors who share my detailed hopes but no surety that what comes next is better.

Mistletoe

The recent polar storm for the ages was frigid air spilling out of the Arctic Circle, plunging into southern latitudes, including Texas with its ostensibly self-sufficient power grid. Rolling blackouts stopped rolling and stalled. Most people lost heat and light. Wearing the warmest clothes they owned, they held each other under heaped blankets in the dark. Some froze to death. Most didn't and emerged four days later into a blighted landscape. Those who wanted—and some of us did because new growth looks hopeful—began to replace trees and plants killed by the record-breaking lows, trees and plants, formerly green, turning brown, then black, emitting smells as they rotted. We queued to enter plant nurseries where staff members kept strict order as grocery store staff members had kept strict order one year earlier during the toilet paper and hand sanitizer shortages. The polar storm arrived during the pandemic but before vaccines, for which we'd also queue.

The polar storm arrived six months after my husband who, while bicycling, was hit by an inattentive driver, and he almost died: obstructed airways on the day of the accident, code red; threatened airways two days later, code orange. Pandemic protocols meant I couldn't see him. Emergency surgery for the threatened airways lasted ten hours, possibly less. Nurses who answered my calls to the trauma unit didn't know because they were busy with everyone's trauma. So he was in the OR for either a ten-hour emergency surgery or for a shorter surgery and the rest of the time in a queue. When he came home, I drove him to specialists. One gave me a flyer, "Patients Who Don't Want Help," and said that these are the patients who heal. My husband walked with a cane, then without, a mile, then two, three, four. I monitored his progress with the phone app that had helped me find him the day of the accident, his location inert that day, no longer coursing across the city as it had been when his bicycle was still moving, not smashed and dropped off outside an ER.

Before the accident I couldn't have known was coming, before the polar storm no one but meteorologists knew was coming, and they knew only days before, my friend and I went for a walk. We headed down sidewalks, then through a sunny vacant lot where she stopped under a solitary tree that looked dead. She pointed at a green cluster in its bare branches. "Mistletoe," she said. She has a PhD in English with an emphasis in ecopoetics, which means seeing the natural world and human thinking as inextricable, which means seeing causality as circular, not linear, which means seeing events not as a one-way chain. Factor A does not cause factor B, nor B cause C, nor C cause D. They cause each other.

Linear causality is more consoling. According to linear logic, you can discern your correct first move and start a train of events in the right direction, toward perpetual ease. According to linear logic, you can look back and isolate your wrong first move and avoid repeating this wrong first move and from now on safeguard against future regret and sorrow.

When my friend pointed at the green cluster in the tall tree, I asked her: "Like Christmas mistletoe?" If I'd have noticed it at all, I'd have thought the tree was putting out last-ditch new shoots, trying to live, not die. She nodded. The tradition of kissing under mistletoe is due to the Druid practice of harvesting mistletoe during the winter solstice because its white-oozing berries were thought to contain the regenerative semen of the gods. Or because, after the son of the Nordic goddess Frigga was restored to life, she made mistletoe a symbol of enduring love. Yet it's a parasite that sucks nutrients, and once I knew what to look for, I started finding it everywhere, on dying trees in the city and on acres of disfigured trees in the country and always that telltale cluster of green, the cause.

You understand, then, that I want a cause. Before the polar storm.

Before the accident.

Before the pandemic.

Before the preceding four years of my "family problems," as I'd learned to vaguely say to avoid questions I'd learned to expect: *wait? what? really?* My daughter had been the target of hate crimes for two years, vandalism, then an assault. For two years, I tried to keep her safe. She moved nearer. Having moved, she seemed safe, but I didn't trust she was. As "family problems" go, hate crimes are so atypical that, when I'd tried to confide, people saying *wait, what?* seemed to hope I'd somehow failed to foresee them.

When I was in the midst of the four years of "family problems," I consulted a new doctor for a flare-up of a chronic illness. His office was being remodeled, soon to be gleaming, modern. For now, it was a run-down suite in an old strip mall, power cords, lumber, and a tipped-over sink in the dark hall leading to a windowless room, all of which were hard not to interpret as warning signs he was a bad doctor. But he rationally asked about my chronic illness, its first onset, which had occurred during a long-ago previous welter of emergencies. Emergencies sometimes coincide. One might make you inept for the others. In that long-ago previous welter of emergencies, my mother had died, my little daughter was sick, and then I got sick. I stopped sleeping during that welter too, as I had during this one. This doctor said: "What about your self-care?" I thought he meant for my illness. "For peace of mind," he added, nonetheless prescribing a biological, or logical, cure.

The first night of shelter in place, I slept for the first time in over six weeks, my long-running insomnia (not counting the dozing near dawn) somehow cured. I'd sometimes dozed near dawn during the previous welter of emergencies, when my mother had died and my little daughter was sick, and a doctor back then said about the not-sleeping back then, "You should have had a psychotic break by now," and I'd answered, "But I don't think I have yet." When shelter in place began, I slept because I didn't have to role-play the next day, to present as normal.

I had more time to walk, first on sidewalks, then on trails, and I'd think *this isn't working*, until I'd be three miles out, three miles to get home, up and down and over hills, steep rocks, bone-conduction headphones streaming music, dissonant chords rising and falling, crying out for solution, and my parasympathetic nervous system cut a mysterious path.

At this time, I was reading a book about objects owned by the Brontës—Charlotte, Emily, and Anne—and it described a walking stick that had belonged to their brother, Branwell, because Emily's walking stick didn't survive or never existed because a walking stick was unseemly for a woman then, as was her compulsive walking. She'd sit in an open window at night, wanting to be outside, because she was aroused out there, loving the moors, stones, and ferns. Many nineteenth-century women loved ferns, their tender, coiling fronds. I started reading this book *before* my husband's accident. I read it for hours the night *after* his accident, when, again, I stopped sleeping. I went night walking, which women don't do now either. Neighbors later told me they'd seen me leave and had texted each other about whether to bring me back inside but didn't. I was sitting on a curb under a tree bewitchingly lit by a streetlamp when the trauma surgeon finally phoned.

At this time, my ecopoetics friend emailed to ask me how I was, and I wrote back that I was believing in best outcomes. I added a paragraph about nineteenth-century fern madness, a collecting craze. Women framed ferns, transplanted them into *aqua vivaria*, made them into symbols of life, also death, spectral ferns stripped of greenery, stems and petioles, skeletal ferns. A Miss Jane Myers fell to her death while gathering ferns on a cliff's edge in Perthshire, Scotland. This is a wild reply to an email asking how I was in the wake of my husband's life-or-death accident, but I recently found it in my sent box, and I sound cogent about ferns, cogent about my husband's prognosis, oblivious to all else. I'd been seized by ferns. "Your daughters, perhaps, have been seized with the prevailing 'Pteridomania,'" Charles Kingsley wrote in 1855, as women ferned for their fern albums.

Oblivious, I turned all my attention to gadgets and strategies for progress, a pill dispenser, a wedge pillow, light meals, help for the patient who didn't want it because he didn't want to be invalided out, not yet. And I didn't want that for him, nor for me, and I found other emails I sent at that time, and they're masterfully cogent, exacting about the minutiae of serial right moves that, I see now, were humdrum ephemera, mere duty, red tape.

After my husband was home, I resumed sleeping, but I woke in early darkness, time to think, and one morning thought how, in astrology, when a duration of upheavals occurs, this is called a transit, a passing-through. Do I believe that? More than I believe that the right amalgam of the four humors—blood, two types of bile, phlegm—incite clarity, industry, amity, courage, or, if they're out of whack, error, anger, apathy, gloom. At least as much as I believe in the Quaker and Jesuit prayers for the safety and health of people I love I find on the internet and read aloud at dawn. At least as much as, pagan-like, I submit to the waxing and waning of light. I've dabbled with positivist-materialism too: facts only, no supernatural cause. But the haunt of prophecy, as Wallace Stevens wrote, persists.

Months into the pandemic, months after the accident, weeks before the extreme weather event, the polar storm, I was hiking. I left the main trail and found myself on a promontory boulder over a dry creek filled with white rocks that had floated downstream in floods and settled in elegant angles of repose. Daybreak sunbeams radiated starlike through low branches. I loved this beautiful place. When I returned a week later, I found a ramshackle fort—one of those forts teenagers build as hideaways from parents—atop the boulder. The teenagers must have been strong, I thought. Because stones they'd lifted from the creek bed to hold up old railroad ties and graffitied plywood were huge. The week before, city trucks had picked up bulk trash from curbs, and the teenagers must have hauled the railroad ties and plywood from the streets, through the woods, down the dry creek bed, up onto the boulder. Teenagers stranded in a pandemic need projects, I decided.

That's not true. I hated that ramshackle fort beyond all reasonable measure.

Hate and love light up the same region of your brain. But logic is deactivated for love, not so much for hate. In love, you take leave of your senses. Hating, you make a plan. I'd deflected my hate. The herd of elephants in my living room did not include a ramshackle fort erected on a promontory boulder over a pearly creek bed dappled in soft light.

A year later, after my free-floating hate for the ramshackle fort had dissipated, I pictured nice teenagers stranded in a pandemic who'd needed a project with what psychologists call "flow," immersion in intricate problem-solving that transforms time. Flow is doing this or that for a partial solution until you glimpse the big solution. Flow is why people like crossword puzzles and cryptograms and TV shows about clues leading to answers. Housework might not be everyone's flow, but for me, tidying sometimes creates flow so mesmerizing my husband once showed me a cartoon of a woman cleaning out the door, down a sidewalk, down a road, and her family tells her to come back, she's cleaned too far.

At this time, I gave myself some flow by bringing a trash bag whenever I hiked, tidying up after pandemic hikers, novices who'd leave their trash behind. I ignored a moldering blanket left in meadow grass, thinking its owners would return for it, but when they didn't after two weeks, I folded it and hid it behind a log. I tried to avoid the side trail leading to the promontory boulder, the site of the ramshackle fort, the site of my hatred, but I didn't have enough willpower. Every time I'd see that ramshackle fort, rage flooded my body. One day, I saw the fort was collapsing, first a propped-up railroad tie, then a plywood wall, then another, until it was an ugly pile. I decided to clear a little each hike.

Since I'm not a strong teenager, clearing meant pushing, one at a time, a railroad tie or plywood sheet to the rockface behind the promontory boulder, hoisting or tilting it. Then I'd climb up or around the rockface and drag it into greenery to hide it. I rolled stones I could budge into the plunge pool at the base of the boulder. Stones too heavy to budge, I left.

I got home from doing this on January 6, 2021, and my husband had the TV on in the middle of the day, live coverage, an extreme event, not weather. The insurrection, as it came to be known, occurred a month before the polar storm, not that I believe timing has hidden meaning, but, according to news reports, the people on TV wielding weapons and costumed as if for Halloween—one of them already killed, others killing—believed in hidden meaning.

Everyone in a pandemic needs flow, I think now. I'm not usually a day drinker. But that day, I drank as the room darkened, sunset. Let go and let vodka. Those people had found flow on YouTube and 4chan, mythically mystical clues leading to their mythically mystical solution, irruption of the historical era that befell four years earlier and caused, at least in part, my family problems about which I don't provide specifics because providing specifics is reliving calamity. I've sealed off that part of my past like a tree seals when a branch breaks off. The sealed-over mark, the cicatrix, is part of the tree forever.

The polar storm arrived on February 14, 2021, and 80 percent of people living in Texas had no heat for four days. Over two hundred froze to death, including a child asleep in his bed next to his brother who somehow didn't die. My husband and I were among the arbitrary few who never lost heat, just water, and we'd bought bottled water at the start of the pandemic a year earlier, and when this ran out, we went outside with bins and buckets and filled a bathtub with snow. We expected to go cold and dark soon, next, but didn't. We awaited, staring out at shrubs and trees and plants and grass layering in white. At night, the world heaved, inhuman noises. Live oaks older than our house, older than our neighborhood, older than most of the city, encrusted with ice, creaked in the astounding cold.

In the thawing days afterward, people forgot.

No one likes remembering extremes. Days immobilized under heavy blankets in the dark. Days of drinking water but not using it to wash. The pandemic was old news, so no reason to reconsider that. Nor the shambolic attempt at a presidential coup. I didn't like to remember, not just yet, worldwide melting glaciers, hurricanes, storms, drought. We queued. Some people lined up to wash their cars. Others to carry water to people who still didn't have any, burst mains. Some to buy seedlings, though nurseries lost power, so seedlings arrived willy-nilly and pricey from out-of-state growers. At this time, a friend, who hopes to be a lifestyle coach, posted a video of herself walking for well-being, talking into her smartphone about the importance of a positive mindset, and I watched, insensible to the message, staring at rows of trees behind her so hurt by the freeze they looked scorched by fire.

Next, we queued for vaccines, in parking lots, auditoriums. My husband, category 1B, was first. We drove two hundred miles for his because, at this time, in cities but not towns, demand exceeded supply. Not knowing what would kill us when, we drove, and I looked for glimmers of regeneration. At home, plants I'd given up for dead stirred. In rows of symmetrical trees, identical trees, some thrived while others died. Shrubs greened unevenly. People cut these down or replaced them. A woman I met had driven to Arkansas to buy new Sandawka viburnums. In my yard, I clipped dead twigs, leaving just the green, skeletal.

Then everyone who wanted vaccines, and not everyone did, got them, and I was between my first and second doses, still clearing the ramshackle fort, hurling a log into woods, when it slipped and cut my hand. I was three miles from home. A bleeding wound should be held above the heart with pressure applied. I walked with both hands over my head, one cut, the other applying pressure. Blood ran down both arms. I'd once noticed while gardening, while lifting soil from bags into pots, that scratches stop bleeding quickly when soil clots over them—soil an apparent antihemorrhagic, I'd decided. In the woods, I put some mud on my cut, which stopped bleeding. At home, I washed and bandaged it.

Five days later, the cut was infected. The doctor, her eyes wide, said: "You did *what*?" She told me that tetanus spores, which I'd associated only with rusty nails, grow in mud. The CDC prohibits tetanus shots two weeks before or after COVID vaccines. She listed the warning signs, spasms, neck stiffness, twinges. She added that if I had tetanus I'd know by now, five days since exposure, and gave me antibiotics. I was getting in my car when she raced out the door and across the parking lot, saying she'd had worrying second thoughts and looked up tetanus, and it turns out that incubation is as long as three weeks, so for three weeks I'd watch for spasms, neck stiffness, twinges. I nodded but knew I wouldn't watch, that three weeks was too long, that not looking for warning signs would be the best use of the rest of my life.

I didn't get tetanus. The wound healed. Memories of the storm, of the days after my husband's accident, the worst of the pandemic, and the worst of the previous four years healed too. By day, I work and walk. At night, I banish thinking about clues and errors I've missed. One day, for flow, I was solving a cryptogram puzzle, encrypted text you decipher by looking for recurring patterns. Solving a cryptogram is solving a problem, spotting patches of what you know for sure and, based on that, guessing what you don't know, and presto, big meaning, the solution. Converting this jumble, meaninglessness, into meaning, I got an inkling that turned out to be correct, and the entire answer fell into place:

Failure is not a single, cataclysmic event. You don't fail overnight. Failure is a few errors in judgment repeated every day.

—JIM ROHN

Who is this Jim Rohn to be so sure!? I wondered. I looked him up. He's a motivational speaker. He advises you to raze obstacles, seize power. But clues and errors you've missed might help with nothing. A retrospective hunt for clues and errors works only on problems subject to individual control.

Rain started falling and fell for days. When it stopped, I went hiking and saw that the creek bed, usually chalk-white but strewn with leaves and branches, was scrubbed sparkling clean. Then I noticed the high-water debris line six feet above the creek bed. The rains had apparently become a flashflood. When I took the side trail to the promontory boulder, I saw that every bit of the ramshackle fort and even rocks—small rocks I'd shoved into the plunge pool and heavy rocks I hadn't been strong enough to shove—had washed away like a hill of beans.

At this time, the oldest trees in my yard, the live oaks, were defying their name. They're meant to be evergreen: never bare. They were bare. The horticultural advice? Wait and hope. Then I spotted in the highest branches of one a telltale cluster of green. How long had it been there? Next, I saw mistletoe in a neighbor's tree. Then, on a country drive, I saw blighted trees and clusters of green, and I said so, and my husband said that at first he'd been interested in the cause of dead trees but by now he was tired of my mistletoe talk. I called a tree surgeon for the tree in my yard, though. By the time he arrived, the tree was budding out lovely, a pale green haze. The tree surgeon climbed up, then back down, and handed me a ball of mistletoe. He said, "You had some, but it isn't always widespread or fatal." As for adages or insight about extreme extremes and violent extremism, that's the best I've got.

ACKNOWLEDGMENTS

Thank you Adrienne Sneed for facilitating insight. Thank you Bethany
Snead. Thank you Susan Harris for deft copyediting. I thank Cecily Parks,
fern-friend, moss-friend, essay-friend. I thank Shen Christenson, my an-
notating great reader. I thank David Meischen for deep insight; Tracy Sta-
ton for her eagle eye; Goldberry Long for the notecard reset; Rahel Girma
Schaeffer for long-running conversation that made shelter in place more
sheltered; and students sometimes so astonishingly risk-taking they inspired me to write differently, especially Bonnie Ilza Cisneros, Rachel
Spies, Taylor Kirby, and Gazzmine Wilkins.

I thank Victoria Smith who understood a late-breaking problem and
solved it.

Thank you to editors of publications in which some of these essays first
appeared, sometimes in different form or with a different title: *Longreads*
("The Wrong Conversations about Hate Activity"), *Southern Review*
("My Taciturn Valentine"), *Rumpus* ("Trouble in Mind"), *The Account*
("The Makeshift Years"), *Diagram* ("Through the Bathroom Window at
Dusk"), *Solstice* ("The COVID Sunday Drives"), *Two Hawks Quarterly* ("A

Formal Feeling"), *North Dakota Quarterly* ("Garnett and the Lavender-Lit Room"), *Air/Light* ("Last Home").

⤎⤏

I acknowledge Gary Kansteiner who, without trying, because he's essentially kind and fair, a great coparent, also smart and interesting, a better husband than I could have invented if I'd been given the magical ability to invent a husband, makes my writing life and entire life better. I acknowledge Marie and Fraiser, who have made me rich in love.

CRUX, THE GEORGIA SERIES IN LITERARY NONFICTION

Debra Monroe, *My Unsentimental Education*

Sonja Livingston, *Ladies Night at the Dreamland*

Jericho Parms, *Lost Wax: Essays*

Priscilla Long, *Fire and Stone: Where Do We Come From?
What Are We? Where Are We Going?*

Sarah Gorham, *Alpine Apprentice*

Tracy Daugherty, *Let Us Build Us a City*

Brian Doyle, *Hoop: A Basketball Life in Ninety-Five Essays*

Michael Martone, *Brooding: Arias, Choruses, Lullabies, Follies, Dirges, and a Duet*

Andrew Menard, *Learning from Thoreau*

Dustin Parsons, *Exploded View: Essays on Fatherhood, with Diagrams*

Clinton Crockett Peters, *Pandora's Garden: Kudzu, Cockroaches, and Other Misfits of Ecology*

André Joseph Gallant, *A High Low Tide: The Revival of a Southern Oyster*

Justin Gardiner, *Beneath the Shadow: Legacy and Longing in the Antarctic*

Emily Arnason Casey, *Made Holy: Essays*

Sejal Shah, *This Is One Way to Dance: Essays*

Lee Gutkind, *My Last Eight Thousand Days: An American Male in His Seventies*

Cecile Pineda, *Entry without Inspection: A Writer's Life in El Norte*

Anjali Enjeti, *Southbound: Essays on Identity, Inheritance, and Social Change*

Clinton Crockett Peters, *Mountain Madness: Found
and Lost in the Peaks of America and Japan*

Steve Majors, *High Yella: A Modern Family Memoir*

Julia Ridley Smith, *The Sum of Trifles*

Siân Griffiths, *The Sum of Her Parts: Essays*

Ned Stuckey-French, *One by One, the Stars: Essays*

John Griswold, *The Age of Clear Profit: Collected Essays on Home and the Narrow Road*

Debra Monroe, *It Takes a Worried Woman: Essays*